ERRANDS
into the
METROPOLIS

ERRANDS
into the
METROPOLIS

New England Dissidents in
Revolutionary London

JONATHAN BEECHER FIELD

DARTMOUTH COLLEGE PRESS
HANOVER, NEW HAMPSHIRE

Published by University Press of New England
Hanover and London

Dartmouth College Press
Published by University Press of New England,
One Court Street, Lebanon, NH 03766
www.upne.com

Printed in the United States of America
5 4 3 2 1

Library of Congress Cataloging-in-Publication Data
Field, Jonathan Beecher.
Errands into the metropolis: New England dissidents in
revolutionary London / Jonathan Beecher Field.
p. cm.—(Reencounters with colonialism—
new perspectives on the Americas)
Includes bibliographical references and index.
ISBN 978-1-58465-774-3 (cloth: alk. paper)
ISBN 978-1-58465-821-4 (pbk.: alk. paper)
1. Rhode Island—History—Colonial period, ca. 1600-1775.
2. Rhode Island—Politics and government—To 1775.
3. Dissenters, Religious—Rhode Island—History.
4. Dissenters, Religious—Political activity—England—History—
17th century. 5. Politics and literature—England—History—
17th century. 6. Discourse analysis—History—17th century.
7. Great Britain—Colonies—Administration—History—
17th century. 8. Great Britain—Colonies—America—History—
17th century. I. Title.
F82.F54 2009
974.5'02—dc22   2009007661

For Daniel Field

London, England . . . consider yourselves . . . warned!

—PUBLIC ENEMY

CONTENTS

ACKNOWLEDGMENTS

The opportunity to acknowledge the many debts I have accumulated in writing this book is one of the greatest joys that comes with finishing it. What is good in this book is largely the responsibility of the names that follow; its limitations and errors are my own. The greatest sorrow that attends finishing this book is not being able to share it with my father, to whom it is dedicated.

Errands into the Metropolis began life as a dissertation in the Department of English Language and Literature at the University of Chicago. I am grateful to my advisor, Janice Knight, as well as Eric Slauter and W. Clark Gilpin of the Divinity School, who were an engaged, challenging, and above all, patient dissertation committee. I also thank Janel Mueller, Richard Strier, and Stephen Pincus for opening my eyes to Tudor and Stuart England. Among my classmates, I am especially grateful to Jon Aronoff, Elisabeth Ceppi, Laura Demanski, and Katie Skeen for their encouragement and support. I owe a debt of thanks to Alice Schreyer for providing me employment during a lean year, and a much greater one for giving me an abiding awareness of the materiality of books.

I had the opportunity to pursue much of the research for this project under the auspices of fellowships at the John Carter Brown Library and the John Nicholas Brown Center for the Study of American Civilization at Brown University. I am grateful to Norman Fiering and his staff at the JCB, especially Susan Newberry, Susan Danforth, and Richard Ring, as well as former JNBC director Joyce Botelho and her staff. At Brown, Jim Egan, Tom Gleason, Philip Gould, and Pat Herlihy helped make Providence a home away from home for an itinerant graduate student. Ed

Lefkowicz and Dan Siegel provided employment, friendship, and a continuing bibliographic education.

In Boston, a grant from the Massachusetts Historical Society allowed me to extend and refine my research. I join many scholars in thanking Peter Drummey, Bill Fowler, and Conrad Wright for their stewardship of this invaluable resource for scholars. I completed the dissertation in Boston, which would have been impossible without the generous cooperation of the member libraries of the Boston Library Consortium, especially the O'Neill Library at Boston College.

My colleagues at Clemson continue to make South Carolina a congenial place to pursue scholarship on colonial New England. I am grateful to Lee Morrissey for showing the way from Boston to Clemson. Catherine Paul and Susanna Ashton have been invaluable mentors and supporters. The support of grants from the Department of English, the College of Art, Architecture and the Humanities, and Clemson University research funds provided the time and space I needed to write this book. More generally, I thank colleagues and students alike for fostering the exciting intellectual environment in Clemson's English department that makes our campus home worthy of its nickname. Outside of the English department, the support of Dr. and Ms. Revis-Wagner and their staff has been indispensable.

Beyond Clemson, a number of scholars have been kind enough to read or to listen to portions and versions of *Errands*. I am grateful to Bernard Bailyn, Joyce Chaplin, Matt Cohen, Elizabeth Maddock Dillon, Jonathan Earle, Karen Kupperman, Ed Larkin, Lynn Rhoads, Dan Richter, Jason Shaffer, Laura Stevens, and Leslie Tuttle, as well as participants in various workshops at the John Carter Brown Library, the John Nicholas Brown Center, the Massachusetts Historical Society, the Society of Early Americanists meetings, the University of Chicago early American workshop, the Georgia early American workshop, as well as the Atlantic Seminar at Harvard and the Futures of American Studies seminar at Dartmouth.

At Dartmouth/UPNE, Don Pease and Richard Pult have been a joy to work with. I am grateful to Michelle Burnham and Jordan Stein for their thoughtful responses to the manuscript for this book. Chris Onstad was generous enough to take a break from Achewood and create the cover.

Belonging to a family of academics has almost always been an asset during my work on this project. The support of aunts, uncles, and cousins, especially Jonathan Beecher, Merike Lapassar-Beecher, Mary and Ren Parker, and Mary and Rick Price, has meant a great deal to me.

Closer to home, my brother Rick, his wife, Susie, and my mother, Holly, have provided more kinds of sustenance than I could begin to name.

The biggest debt of gratitude I owe is to Amy Monaghan. She was in a car with me on the way to Quebec City when I babbled out the first inchoate version of this project. That she is with me to see this final version fills me with joy. She has read many parts of this book in many versions over many years—the struggle to write this paragraph without recourse to her eye and ear suggests how much her help has meant to *Errands*. However, if she had never read a word of this book, she would still be the most important reason for finishing it.

ERRANDS
into the
METROPOLIS

INTRODUCTION

I

In 1663, Charles II, the restored king of England, granted a charter to the colony of Rhode Island and Providence Plantations. The king put his seal to several colonial charters in the early years of his reign, but the charter for Rhode Island was unusual. Unlike similar charters for Connecticut and Massachusetts granted after the Restoration, the political status Charles II gave Rhode Island was not a royal confirmation of a colony originally chartered under the reign of an earlier Stuart monarch. In designating the citizens of Rhode Island "a bodye politique or corporate," the king gave political legitimacy to a collection of settlements that owed their legal existence to privileges granted by various Parliamentary bodies, after they had seized power from Charles II's father, Charles I.[1]

This collection of settlements was also unusual. In contrast to the typical pattern for founding English colonies in North America, the settlements forming Rhode Island existed in fact in America before they existed in law in England. Roger Williams founded Providence after his Separatist principles led to his expulsion from Massachusetts; Anne Hutchinson's party founded the island settlements of Portsmouth and Newport in the aftermath of the Antinomian Controversy; Samuel Gorton (called a familist by his enemies but defying easy description) settled Warwick after running afoul of several New England governments.[2] Against the model of a royal grant of a patent or charter for a swath of North America creating an abstraction that colonists would subsequently fulfill, this charter conferred unified political recognition to a heterogeneous collection of settlements founded under duress by refugees and exiles from more established colonies.

Every settlement forming the colony chartered as Rhode Island and Providence Plantations had either legal or voluntary exiles from the Massachusetts Bay Colony for founders. Given the vexed relations these settlers had with their more orthodox colonial neighbors, it is not surprising that the 1663 Rhode Island charter came only as the culmination of a series of struggles by Rhode Islanders to forestall efforts by the Massachusetts Bay Colony, as well as Plymouth and Connecticut, to seize the territory these dissidents occupied.[3] In 1644, Roger Williams sailed home from London with the first charter for Rhode Island and Providence Plantations, despite the competing claims of Thomas Weld and Hugh Peter on behalf of Massachusetts. Samuel Gorton followed Williams's example in 1646 by securing a Parliamentary order confirming his tenure on Shawomet Neck, which he renamed Warwick. He prevailed in this errand over Edward Winslow, who presented the Bay Colony's case against Gorton to London readers. In 1652, John Clarke, a Baptist, successfully petitioned Cromwell's Council of State to rescind Bay Colony sympathizer William Coddington's effort to take the government of Portsmouth and Newport into his own hands. The grant of the 1663 charter, which was also Clarke's doing, followed another defeat for Massachusetts interests in the court of Charles II: In 1661, the king issued a writ preventing Massachusetts from resorting to capital punishment against Quakers who used Rhode Island as a base for their forays into the less tolerant precincts of Massachusetts, Plymouth, Connecticut, and New Haven.

In sum, an illustrated map of Rhode Island at the time of the Restoration would look rather like a real-life colonial version of the frontispieces that appeared in some of the editions of Ephraim Pagitt's *Heresiography* published around this time, with images of Seekers, Familists, Antinomians, and Anabaptists.[4]

Charters, patents, and boundaries are usually the province of history, rather than literature. However, *Errands into the Metropolis* is not a history of colonial Rhode Island. Indeed, Rhode Island, in itself, is not fundamental to the concerns of this project. Instead, this project considers the struggles to control Rhode Island and their outcomes as evidence supporting an argument about the unique possibilities confronting colonial authors writing for English audiences in the middle of the seventeenth century. The flows of power and knowledge between colony and metropolis created distinct opportunities for colonial dissidents to make appeals

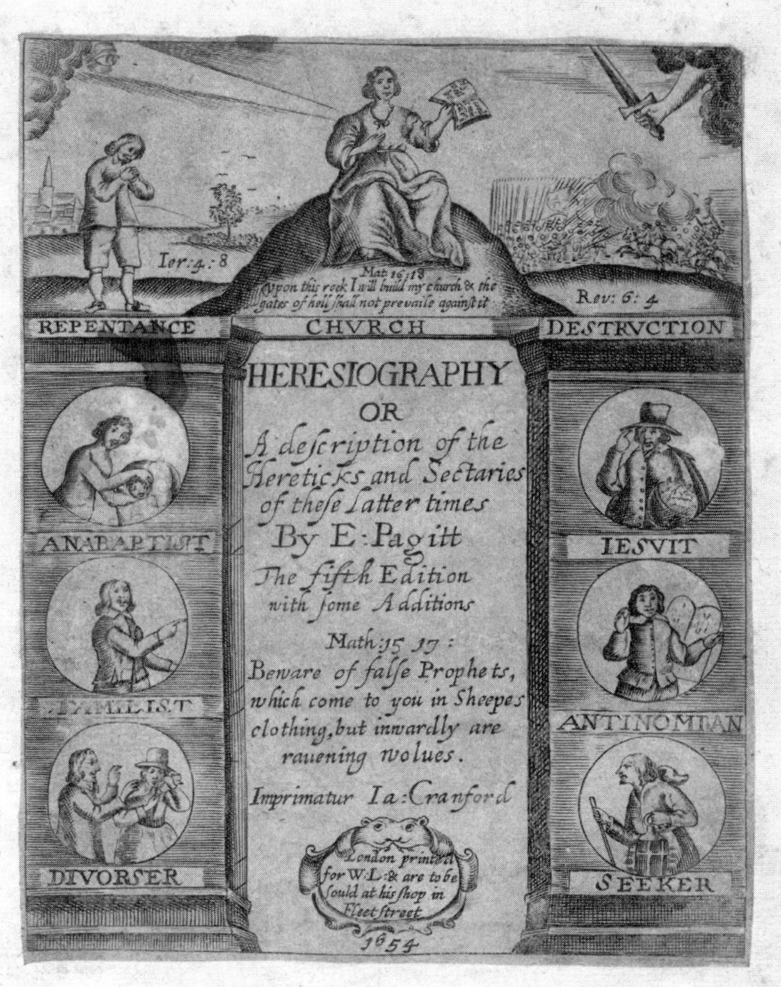

FIGURE 1: Title page, Ephraim Pagitt, *Heresiography* (London: 1654).
*Courtesy of Houghton Library, Harvard College Library *EC P1483 645hg.*

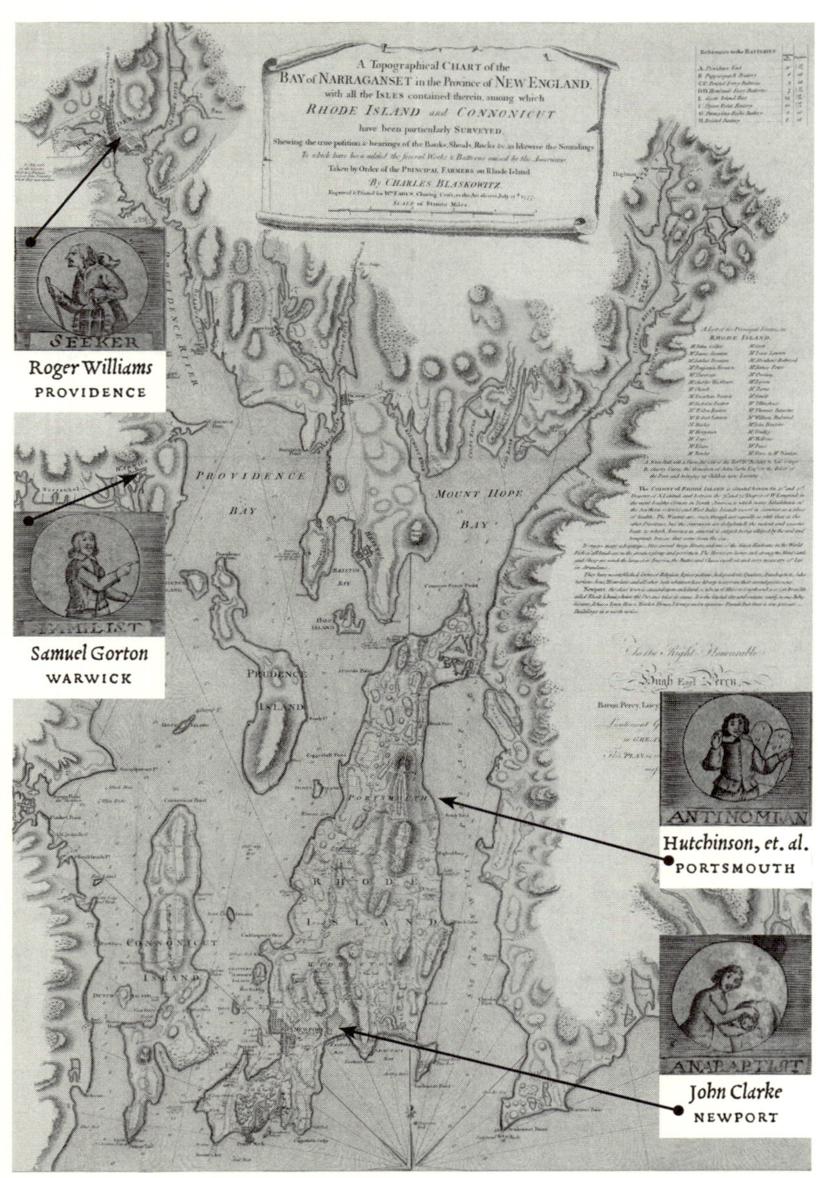

FIGURE 2: Map of Rhode Island,
showing settlement locations of dissident groups.
Courtesy of the John Carter Brown Library.

to metropolitan authority in the form of printed texts. As David Zaret details, New Englanders joined their domestic brethren in participating in the new discursive milieu created by the explosion of print: "Printing in the English Revolution pushed political communication in new directions that today we associate with public opinion."[5] Zaret argues that print imposes a dialogic form on these debates, which appeal to a nascent form of public opinion. If anything, writers from New England enjoyed an additional degree of freedom in their appeals. By framing their stories in ways that resonated with literary forms familiar to metropolitan readers, colonial dissidents availed themselves of specific discursive opportunities produced by a historically distinct combination of political, cultural, and technological circumstances.

The space between the colonies and London warranted written narrations of disputes from the concerned parties, which metropolitan authorities had to adjudicate at a great remove from any direct contact with the issue in question. Thus, the state of communications technology at this time makes a literary analysis of these debates not just possible, but essential. The mechanisms of seventeenth-century colonial power required colonial disputes to be adjudicated textually, and thus required written narratives from the concerned parties in the dispute. To a degree, then, rhetorical ability in print could place an overmatched political dissident or religious radical on equal footing with antagonists with far greater coercive power at their disposal. The success of these Rhode Island dissidents in London shows how they could transmute participation in English print culture into political authority in New England.

Rhode Island's persistent survival is evidence of the power of print in the Atlantic world. The form of the appeals dissidents carried to London was also the medium of the reciprocating colonial governance—the written word. Of a later English colonial project, Homi Bhabha observes that in nineteenth-century India, "If the spirit of the Western nation has been symbolized in epic and anthem, voiced by 'a unanimous people assembled in the self-presence of its speech,' then the sign of colonial government is cast in a lower key, caught in the irredeemable act of writing."[6] Writing of the earliest documents of the colonial encounter, Myra Jehlen observes, "America was conceived under the sign of the printing press."[7] The ocean separating New England and London meant that words could cross in one direction as complaints or appeals, and return in the other with the force of law. For the mid-seventeenth century, it might be more accurate to say that America was constantly re-conceived under the sign of the printing press.

Thus, control of Providence, Warwick, Aquidneck, and Rhode Island as a whole are the stakes of a broader ideological contest that took place in London, enacted in print between religious dissidents and their more orthodox opponents. Understanding the success of these dissidents is important to any understanding of seventeenth-century New England, for these efforts by dissidents to defend the grounds they occupied from the ideological and territorial ambitions of their neighbors had lasting impacts on the culture, history, and boundaries of New England. *Errands into the Metropolis* shows how a succession of New England dissidents were able to travel to metropolitan London, recount their sufferings at the hands of the more orthodox governments of New England, and use these narratives to secure autonomy for their own settlements from a succession of English colonial authorities.

The success of these dissidents is as dramatic in its English context as in its North American context. These dissidents were not only at odds with the established religious authorities in New England, but also outside the main currents of religious opinion at home in London. These appeals are from a diverse array of religious dissidents to a diverse array of bodies charged with overseeing England's colonies. To be sure, the spectrum of opinion was broader in London than in Boston, but none of these dissidents embraced a faith that would, on its own merits, attract powerful political support in London. Moreover, reliable sources of political support could be difficult to locate when power was shifting so rapidly in London. The years when dissidents made these appeals were violent and tumultuous ones in England, and the changes in government had corresponding effects on the various bodies charged with the supervision of the colonies. Neither the religion of the petitioners, nor the political orientation of their auditors, adequately explains the political success of these religious dissidents.

The explanation for the success of these dissidents lies not in England or in North America, but with the ocean that separates them. Specifically, the state of navigation and print technology in this period rendered the printed metropolitan word the authoritative version of actual colonial experience. The success Williams, Gorton, Clarke, and the Quakers enjoyed indicates that in the early years of England's colonization of North America, the nature of the relation between colony and metropolis offered unusual opportunities to dissidents who would otherwise be marginal figures on either side of the Atlantic. The particular way print could link New England and England allowed a succession of colonists expelled from the more orthodox New England colonies to retain their hold on a southeastern corner of New England, where they gained political autonomy and unprecedented religious latitude united as the colony of Rhode Island and Providence Plantations.

Speaking broadly, in each of these cases, the Bay Colony persecutes religious dissidents, who travel to London to tell their stories of persecution. In London, this story finds sufficient resonance with whichever body of colonial overseers is in power at that moment that they grant the dissidents a political instrument guaranteeing the colonial autonomy of their own settlement, and protecting their party from further sufferings at the hands of the Massachusetts Bay Colony and its allies. The case of the Quakers departs from this pattern only by extending this model to involve the coordinated efforts of like-minded religious dissidents on both sides of the Atlantic, and by eliciting an order that stayed the hand of the Bay Colony within its own borders, rather than frustrating its ambitions to extend them.[8] These cases, to be sure, do not include all of those who dissented from the New England Way. John Child, Thomas Lechford, and, most notably, Anne Hutchinson did not manage to carve out a space for their dissident views. In the cases of Child and Lechford, the stakes of their arguments with the Bay Colony were ideological, and lacked a territorial claim that an adjudicating body could honor or not.

Anne Hutchinson's case is more complicated. She is a more prominent dissenting voice in New England than any of the dissidents this book treats in detail, with the possible exception of Roger Williams. She is, however, primarily a voice—her words reach us in the context of trial transcripts prepared by her antagonists, not in texts where she has an authorial claim.[9] It is certainly possible to instrumentalize gender as the factor that allows Williams, Gorton, and Clarke access to print, and denies it to Hutchinson, but the actual circumstance seems slightly more complicated. As an opponent of the Bay Colony's theocracy, Hutchinson enjoyed the same access to colonial print that Williams, Gorton, and Clarke did, which is to say, none at all. The few publications that issued from the Bay Colony's press served the cause of orthodoxy, and nothing resembling a free press was available at this time. In order to have access to print, the dissidents from Rhode Island needed to have the means to travel to London and publish their dissent there. What reception Hutchinson might have gotten in London is hard to discern (there were, to the consternation of observers like Thomas Edwards, female publishers and preachers in London in the 1640s), but as Hutchinson was unwilling or unable to make the trip, we cannot know the answer to this question.

It may well be that the demands of her family prevented her from making the kind of trip that Williams, Gorton, and Clarke made, but as the case of Mary Dyer and her fellow Quakers demonstrates, it was not necessary for the victim of persecution to travel in person to the metropolis for their narrative to be heard. If Hutchinson's Antinomian followers had managed even a rudimentary form of the network Quakers developed, Hutchinson's Antinomian followers might have gained the kind of legal foothold in Rhode Island that their neighbors achieved.

II

The question of how Rhode Island happened, despite the checkered pedigrees of its founders, and despite the ambitions of its Puritan neighbors for the ground it occupied, is of more than local interest. Rhode Island's small size makes it tempting to dismiss its survival with a shrug, and some scholars have favored this approach. Philip Gura, whose *Glimpse of Sion's Glory* is the only major book-length study of New England heterodoxy, argues that dissidents, including Rhode Island's founders, were an inoculant against a broader disintegration of consensus, thus promoting cohesion among more orthodox New Englanders. Describing the challenges that Roger Williams, Anne Hutchinson, and the Quakers posed to the New England Way, Gura asserts, "between 1630 and 1660, the doctrinal and ecclesiastical, as well as imaginative, development of American Puritanism was nurtured in soil thoroughly turned by the radical elements in the New Englanders' midst."[10] Especially considering that Williams discusses the parable of the wheat and the tares in the *Bloudy Tenent,* this is a curious metaphor Gura uses, in its image of American Puritanism flourishing in a field tilled by dissidents.

In a similar vein, Stephen Foster's rich and nuanced study of the transatlantic evolutions of the Puritan movement recapitulates this marginalization in the context of Quakers, who "made their converts in New England mainly in the familiar places on the geographical periphery of orthodoxy, where the mechanisms for inculcating the Puritan message were absent, or unusually impaired: in Rhode Island, in Kittery in Maine, on Long Island, far out on Cape Cod in Plymouth Colony, in pockets of endlessly festering, ever-combustible Salem."[11] In an earlier article, Foster shares Gura's notion of the services of dissent to orthodoxy: "The successive invasions of New England launched by the Gortonists, the Baptists, and the Quakers after 1640 were the less formidable for being better defined than the illusive 'Familism' of the Hutchinsonians, but in any case their failure had already been predetermined by the events of the 1630s: their strongest appeals were blunted in advance by the semisectarian innovations made in the New England Way in the latter part of the decade."[12]

Gura's and Foster's readings of the relation between dissent and orthodoxy make sense in the context of a particular spatial imaginary, one where New England exists as a more or less cohesive cultural field. However, the image of "successive invasions" is misleading, if it suggests that Gortonists, Baptists, and Quakers sought to plant their flag on Beacon Hill, were repelled, and retreated to a Rhode Island beachhead. To be sure, in the early decades of settlement, the Bay Colony theocracy generally succeeded in maintaining what Perry Miller called "orthodoxy in Massachusetts," but Rhode Island dissidents also managed to construct a space where they could live and worship in their own terms. From a dissident perspective, this freedom, not control of Winthrop's City on a Hill, is the more significant issue.

Maintaining these settlements that became Rhode Island as heterodox spaces in the heart of New England did not require palisades and muskets, but rather an ongoing transatlantic renegotiation of the fundamental premises of the English presence in New England. Appreciating the structure, content, and outcome of the colonial conflicts that had control of portions of Rhode Island as their stakes offers several rewards for scholars of early America and the Atlantic world. In terms of early American historiography, understanding the survival of these dissenting political entities contributes to an ongoing effort to replace models emphasizing orthodoxy and consensus as the essence of colonial New England. Such views, of course, owe their prominence to Perry Miller's foundational work in *Orthodoxy in Massachusetts* and *The New England Mind*, but in the intervening years, many have found his conception of the New England mind uncomfortably narrow. The title of Janice Knight's *Orthodoxies in Massachusetts* is emblematic of this development, as is its delineation of two significantly divergent schools of thought within the putatively monolithic mainstream of New England Puritanism.

The narrower view persists, not only in a popular sense of colonial New England as a repressive, "Puritanical" place, but also in some recent scholarship. In his study of the evolution of toleration, Andrew Murphy notes, "The Massachusetts Bay Colony has long been viewed as perhaps the quintessential example of a colonial regime that during its early years effectively suppressed claims to religious toleration and liberty of conscience."[13] This view persists in more recent work, such as Darren Staloff's application of the sociology of intellectuals to colonial New England to explain the "cultural domination" of Boston's ministers and magistrates.[14]

However, other scholars have challenged older models of New England's early history that emphasize consensus, even as Early American Studies as a whole has moved away from New England as the primary field of study. For early American studies at large, both of these developments have proved salutary. Within a New England context, works like Foster's *Long Argument* and Knight's *Orthodoxies in Massachusetts* enrich and complicate the understandings of intellectual life in New England articulated by previous generations of scholars.[15] Lisa Gordis's *Opening Scripture* demonstrates that the scriptural authority at the foundation of this society was itself contested and ambiguous.[16] So, too, the increased attention to the mid-Atlantic Chesapeake, Deep South, and Caribbean is good news for early Americanists of all stripes, but the focus on these regions has left unfinished business in New England.

The impetus among many early Americanists to explore other regions besides New England comes from an awareness that New England is not equivalent to America: A worldview where Plymouth, Massachusetts, is "America's Hometown" leaves many Americans out of the story. However, this equation of a part with a whole mirrors the same phenomenon occurring within New England, where "New England" stands for Massachusetts, and, more specifically, an elite population in Boston. With few exceptions, the constitutive elements of Perry Miller's "New England Mind" lived, worked, and preached along the banks of the Charles River. However, the success of religious dissidents from outside this region indicates that in London, "New England" was not simply shorthand for "Massachusetts," or an elite group centered around Boston, suggesting instead that London print culture provided the medium for ongoing debates on the nature and structure of New England.[17] By considering how colonial texts construct New England in London print culture, texts that frequently garner only superficial notice in the literature warrant new and sustained analysis. Samuel Gorton's *An Incorruptible Key Composed of the 110th Psalm* (1647), for instance, a work that has escaped scholarly scrutiny almost entirely, takes on a new significance for its radical reconfiguration of John Cotton's ministry for London readers. In a dedicatory epistle, Gorton claims the work is an effort to redeem John Cotton's cack-handed attempt to explicate the same psalm, quoting a letter purportedly from his adherents in Boston:

> Since your departure from amongst us, M. John Cotton, Teacher of the Church of Boston, hath taken occasion to expound the hundred and tenth psalme, in the reading of it, wee thought there were divers glimpses of that light which shineth in our lord Jesus appeared unto us. But in his handling of it, and glosses which he gave upon it, we thought the light and truth of our Christ was rather darkened and obscured by him, then any wayes cleared and brought forth in the church.[18]

It is unlikely that Gorton received any such missive, but the Atlantic world in the mid-seventeenth century was a place where he could make such a claim in print confident that it would be months before anyone could challenge it. The position of a New England dissident is legible as the intersection of two emerging views of print culture. Zaret's focus on dialogic order as a constitutive element of the print culture of the 1640s is helpful, but not sufficient, to explain the circumstances that obtained for the likes of Gorton. Models of authorship, or the public sphere, that either presume or explicitly engage a metropolitan milieu do not fully explain the situation of an author who lives on one side of the Atlantic and publishes on the other, so a model that inhabits a broader physical space is necessary. In particular, Trish Loughran's *The Republic in Print* demonstrates a concern with the materiality of print culture in eighteenth- and nineteenth-century America that casts the most fundamental texts of that era in a new light. As Loughran demonstrates, disseminating the print that is the substance of print culture posed a variety of actual, physical challenges in a sprawling continental space like North America, rather than in a concentrated metropolitan space like London.

To this end, Loughran rehearses the experiences of one Hugh Findlay, a British postal employee dispatched to inspect the King's Post Road.[19] His journey is as fraught and picaresque as the more familiar journey of Madam Knight a few decades earlier, but seeing these experiences mediated through the narrative of a postal agent emphasizes the "noncorrespondence and nonsimultaneity" characterizing textual circulation in the early United States. In particular, the bitter experience of Thomas Paine reveals the pitfalls of imagining an idealized, nationalized public sphere as the milieu of *Common Sense*.[20] At the same time, Loughran demonstrates that the noncorrespondence and nonsimultaneity of American print culture was in fact critical to what work print could do before and after the American Revolution. Representation, either political or textual, depends on a spatial and temporal dislocation.[21] A Federal government would be untenable without the kind of dispersion that frustrated Hugh Findlay.

This dislocation opens up a space between readers and writers. In the colonial context, it is a different form of this "noncorrespondence and nonsimultaneity" that allows dissident narrators to construct alternate forms of New England reality in revolutionary London. The dialogic disorder that attends a print debate when one antagonist is on the scene in London and the other is in New England is critical to the success of New England dissidents.

The literary freedom colonial residents publishing in the metropolis enjoyed mirrors the challenges New Englanders remaining in New England faced in conveying their narratives to the metropolis. It is an oversimplification to understand the struggles over pieces of Rhode Island as between dissidents writing in the metropolis and more orthodox apologists writing from the colonies, but we will see that dissidents did more to frame their appeals in contexts that were legible to metropolitan readers than did their rivals. Conversely, Bay Colony apologists wrote from a more provincial perspective, and generally struggled to capture the imagination of metropolitan readers. Dissident appeals succeed expressly at the expense of Massachusetts and over its protests, suggesting that the ideological sway of New England's Puritan colonies was rather feeble and contingent. If Bay Colony apologists like John Cotton, Edward Winslow, and John Norton could not displace the constructions of New England forwarded by the likes of Williams, Gorton, and Clarke, then scholars of this period need to rethink the work of colonial literature in the Atlantic world.

Pushing Zaret's work west geographically, and Loughran's back chronologically, we find, in debates over the constitution of New England, a culture of print dependent on spatial friction, like Loughran's, and inhabiting a seventeenth-century time frame, like Zaret's. Beyond extending one argument in space and another in time, this nexus raises some significant questions for scholars interested seventeenth-century New England. Most immediately, this perspective puts pressure on the archive that Perry Miller and his heirs rest their arguments upon, in making their claims about the more or less magisterial architectonics of the New

England Mind. Overwhelmingly, these are arguments made from books, and books composed on one side of the Atlantic and published on the other. As we will see in the case of John Cotton, and as was true of his fellow clergy, authorship for New England divines was a complicated business. Recognizing that the texts available for the study of New England clergy are products of a vexed and contingent material process enriches our understanding of this culture at large, but also suggests the challenges facing the intellectual historian working in this field. More generally, that the literal constitution, and indeed the very meaning, of New England could be so vigorously contested so far from its shores indicates that any reference to "New England" in the seventeenth century warrants a careful explication of who is articulating this particular New England, and where, when, and to whom they are making this claim.

In a broader context, then, *Errands into the Metropolis* uses the insights of scholars of American and English print culture to consider how print worked in the seventeenth-century Atlantic world. In this context, I hope to engage with the rich tradition of Atlantic studies scholarship that has emerged in recent years. More specifically, however, *Errands* considers the impact that the material conditions of transatlantic authorship can have on Atlantic print culture. A discursive formation that has a large, wet, and stormy ocean as its field works differently than a discursive formation located in neighborhoods of booksellers and coffee shops.

To this end, *Errands into the Metropolis* aims to reconfigure prevailing notions of core and periphery in the seventeenth-century Atlantic world, in both ideological and geographical senses. In the intellectual historiography of New England, the figures I discuss play a small part. Clarke's and Gorton's texts are at best the province of orals reading lists for graduate students, while earlier scholars often framed Williams's achievement in isolation from that of his New England peers, as a proto-Enlightenment prophet of liberty of conscience. Early New England Quakers appear in Quaker historiography, but in narratives of Massachusetts, they figure as a passing crisis, ending with the death of Mary Dyer.[22] English metropolitan audiences, however, read the works of these figures and took them seriously—more seriously, frequently, than those of the Bay Colony's apologists.

Investigating the conditions that permitted Rhode Island's survival reveals discursive circumstances that shaped all of New England's culture in the decades after settlement, not just dissident narratives. English settlers did not create New England with one decisive errand into the wilderness. Rather, English subjects who found themselves in New England constructed the history, boundaries, and culture of New England through a series of errands into the metropolis, where they negotiated and debated the past, present, and future of their new home.

These errands took place between 1643, when Roger Williams secured the first Providence patent, and 1663, when John Clarke secured the Rhode Island charter that served as the frame of government for the colony and state of Rhode Island and Providence Plantations until 1843. This period of these appeals overlaps with the Civil War, Commonwealth, Protectorate, and Restoration in England. These are also years when metropolitan control of American colonies was at its most diffuse and abstract. Beyond the distractions at home in London, these are also the years between the original grants of the charters that shaped the initial character of colonial settlements, and Charles II's appointment of royal commissioners and governors, which worked to enact the wishes of a metropolitan government, often against the will of a colonial populace.[23] The limited power any metropolitan body had over affairs in New England was difficult and tedious to enact; moreover, in the absence of any metropolitan agents, any overseeing body in London supervised by sifting through competing claims that were difficult to compare or evaluate.

Of course, the same politicians who oversaw the colonies had other, much more pressing business in these years, and could devote only limited and sporadic attention to mediating colonial complaints.[24] As such, one can imagine the situation of colonial governance in the years stretching from the initial grants of charters by James I and Charles I, to the appointment of royal commissioners by Charles II and James II, as akin to an adult mediating the quarrels of children in the back seat of a station wagon while driving through heavy traffic. The driver cannot turn around and see the situation firsthand, and must attempt to determine a just solution by appraising the conflicting accounts of the quarreling children.

As a result, metropolitan authorities governed by hearsay: In the absence of a formal system to monitor what was going on in the colonies, colonial overseers were forced to rely on whatever reports happened to reach them, and to make judgments as their limited time and attention allowed. The hearing and saying that hearsay entails involves two technological developments—print and navigation. Sailing ships and printing presses could transform colonial experience into metropolitan expression, even without the presence of the author in the metropolis. As we will see, however, under the best of circumstances, the passage from New England event to London text was both tedious and capricious.

From a colonial perspective, however, the epistemic challenges of administering colonies with such sketchy and imprecise tools of communication rendered the metropolis an offshore public sphere for colonists, where the history, constitution, and existence of various colonies could be debated. In her reading of Weld and Winthrop's *A Short Story of the Rise, Reign, and Ruine of Antinomians, Familists and Libertines,* Elizabeth Maddock Dillon observes that Winthrop's very notion of the Bay Colony "as a 'city on a hill' spells out the Puritan mission in terms that rely upon the notion of a transatlantic public sphere."[25] This concern for their English audience means that Massachusetts Bay "colonists did indeed pay mind to the reports of the colony that reached England, yet they were not ultimately able to control the flow of information across the ocean."[26] Because of this lack of control, dissidents could present their version of events in New England in the metropolis. As an additional advantage, the distance between old and New England meant dissidents could present a different version of New England reality without having to overcome a significant accretion of empirical or ideological received notions about the situation there. Grantland Rice describes this phenomenon as "a unique exchange of transatlantic civic criticism"; beyond this dialogue, it is also a London discursive formation with the power to create facts on the ground in New England.[27]

The discursive space created by this offshore public sphere allows dissidents to re-imagine some of the most basic aspects of the English colonial project. In particular, two themes overlap in dissident narratives: representations of Native Americans as civil or specifically English subjects, and representations of suffering English subjects. Williams and Gorton make appeals that depend upon the notion of the Native American as a civil subject; from this basis, Clarke and the Quakers make appeals that depend upon the image of the English subject unjustly persecuted in the colonies. Thus, the English subjectivity that Charles II endorses with the charter has a Native American source.

Considering colonial New England from this perspective opens up avenues of inquiry that extend beyond colonial historiography. In particular, the religious latitude these dissidents secure with this charter from Charles II also reshapes the context in which we see the ideals of toleration and liberty of conscience emerging. Examining metropolitan responses to colonial persecution reveals toleration emerging as a policy as a pragmatic response to local conflicts, rather than as a deliberate effort to achieve an abstract good. While the degree of religious latitude enjoyed by Rhode Islanders in 1663 was almost without precedent, it was an ideal that emerged dialectically, as a way for a metropolitan power to manage religious differences in far-off colonies. The notion of Roger Williams as some sort of proto-Jeffersonian Enlightenment thinker has passed out of serious scholarship, but it is worth considering what happens to our understanding of toleration if it is a pragmatic response to the material challenges of colonial administration.

In the case of Rhode Island, toleration was significant not only as a right of its citizens, but also as a necessary condition of its existence. Rhode Island appeared and survived as a heterogeneous and autonomous colony despite being tucked between three theocratic colonies hostile to its very existence. *Errands into the Metropolis* traces the development of a discursive circuit that allowed dissident colonists to renegotiate their status with metropolitan authorities. The discursive opportunities afforded by the temporal and spatial distances of the colonial Atlantic world allowed a specific kind of dissenting narrative to evolve. When dissidents circulated these narratives in metropolitan London, they transformed the experience of colonial persecution into the political entity Charles II chartered as Rhode Island and Providence Plantations.

1. 50% Cotton

Authorship, Authority, and the Atlantic

"I never said half the things I said."

—YOGI BERRA, ATTRIB.

I: The Cotton-Williams Debate?

The first dissident errand from New England to London was Roger Williams's 1643–44 trip to London. Roger Williams began and ended his this trip by publishing works concerning Indians. However, *A Key into the Language of America* (1643) and *Christenings Make Not Christians* (1645) bracket a more extensive body of work concerned with English affairs.[1] Of these texts, the *Bloudy Tenent of Persecution* (1644) is the most prominent. *The Bloudy Tenent*, along with *Mister Cotton's Letter Lately Printed Examined and Answered* (1644), are Roger Williams's early salvos in what scholars call the Cotton–Williams debate.[2]

This debate is one of the chestnuts of seventeenth-century American studies. Excerpts from the texts forming the debate are a staple of anthologies covering early America, and interpretations of the debate serve as a principal point of contention between Perry Miller's and Sacvan Bercovich's readings of American Puritanism. In more recent scholarship, the Cotton–Williams debate remains a focus for scholars concerned with questions of toleration and the relation of church and state in seventeenth-century Puritanism.[3]

However, the important issues Cotton and Williams air in this debate can distract readers from its peculiar form. The phrase "Cotton–Williams debate" suggests a figurative, if not literal, discursive field where the protagonists encounter one another and conduct this exchange of ideas. However, this presumption distorts the nature of this debate. It is a debate in that Cotton and Williams disagree, but is not a debate in the sense that its texts are the artifact of an encounter, or even a series of texts simulating an encounter in print. In *The Origins of Democratic Culture*, David Zaret identifies the "imposition of dialogic order on conflict" as a key element in the development of public opinion, which in turn is a constitutive element of the political public sphere [that] first appeared in the English Revolution."[4] According to Zaret, this imposition is a "consequence of increased ability swiftly and massively to reproduce texts." This facility, in turn, led ideological antagonists to the "simultaneous constitution and invocation of public opinion."[5]

Print imposes a the appearance of a "dialogic order" on the texts of the debate, but attention to the material contexts of the Cotton–Williams debate reveals that it was a radically asymmetric conflict. Williams used his presence in the metropolis to provoke the debate and dictate its terms, while Cotton struggled to reply in a meaningful or timely way from the shores of Massachusetts. The difference between the two men's access to print shaped the form of the debate, which in turn influenced its content. More generally, attention to the physical form of this debate reveals how little control the most influential theologian in New England had over the words that appeared in his name. This lack of authorial control is the rule, rather than the exception, for Cotton, and it is a challenge Cotton's brethren faced as well.

This asymmetry is a consistent and critical feature of the printed debates between colonists published in metropolitan London. The reason for this imbalance lies in the same tension between the two senses of the word "errand" that animates Perry Miller's "Errand into the Wilderness." Miller seizes on the difference between an errand one performs for another, and an errand one performs for oneself. "Originally, as the word first took form in English, it meant exclusively a journey on which an inferior is sent to convey a message or perform a service for his superior . . . . But by the end of the Middle Ages, errand developed another connotation: it came to mean the actual business on which the actor goes, the purpose itself."[6] For an aspiring author resident in New England during the first decades of settlement, publishing involved one or the other of these senses of errand. Colonial authors could travel to London to publish on their own behalf, or they could entrust their manuscripts to others. There was, of course, a colonial press after 1639, but it was neither used much nor of much use in contexts like the Cotton–Williams debate. Winning the hearts and minds of London readers was not an office of the provincial press. Thanks to nationalist and antiquarian traditions in bibliography, scholars of early America are familiar with the Freeman's Oath and the *Bay Psalm Book* as the first works to issue from New England presses.[7] But these books are prominent precisely because of they are anomalous American imprints—throughout the seventeenth century, London imprints dominated the shelves of New Englanders, and carried the vast majority of the printed discourse about New England read on both sides of the Atlantic.

The digital edition of the Evans catalog of American imprints lists forty-two imprints for the years 1630 to 1660. *Early English Books Online*, the digital successor to such bibliographies as Wing and Pollard, lists 39,882 items for the same period. *European Americana*, which catalogs books printed in Europe related to the Americas, lists 4,937.[8] Beyond these crude quantitative measures, there is also a qualitative dimension—the majority of New England imprints were utilitarian documents, rather than intellectual interventions. Among these forty-two are eleven Harvard thesis announcements, nine almanacs, four works related to evangelizing Indians, and four catechisms. By contrast, only two sermons and one other theological work appear on the list, along with John Norton's *Heart of N-England Rent* (1659), an anti-Quaker tract. Also, if reaching a broad audience is part of the reason for publishing, then publishing for the small New England readership amounted to a print version of the sort of coterie publication Philip Round describes in a scribal context.[9]

Instead, publishing in England was the rule for New England theologians like Cotton. After his migration to America in 1633, John Cotton never returned to England, yet, during his lifetime, none of the thirty-six titles of which he was the primary author was published in America.[10] Thus, everything that appeared under his name after from his migration to his death, and beyond, was the product of an errand performed by someone else. These errands, however, did not require Cotton's consent, or even his cognizance. Even under the best of circumstances, his manuscripts faced a long series of intermediate steps, which could delay, distort, or discredit his pronouncements.

More particularly, the exchange between Cotton and Williams is a phenomenon of involuntary authorship, for Cotton did not ask for this debate, even though he appears to initiate it. In fact, the two exchanges comprising the debate began as two separate fights picked in print by Williams. Cotton's letter to Williams ostensibly opens the debate, but he had written this letter to Williams long ago, in New England. Williams's supporters in London were evidently behind its appearance in London, choosing to disseminate it in the metropolis beyond its colonial audience of one.[11] It appeared late in 1643, while *Mr. Cotton's Letter Examined* appeared early in 1644, suggesting perhaps that Williams had prepared his response ahead of time and released it after the "accidental" publication of *Mr. Cotton's Letter*.[12] If Williams did not convey this letter to the press himself, it is hard to imagine how this letter could appear without his connivance. Not only would Williams have to make the letter available to whomever did carry it to the press, but he would have needed to bring it with him from Providence.

Similarly, the *Bloudy Tenent* takes the form of an extended commentary on Cotton's 1635 commentary on a 1620 letter from an imprisoned Anabaptist. The remainder of the work is largely a critique of "A Model of Church and Civil Power," which Williams claims was delivered by Cotton and others to the church at Salem, but survives only in the portions of it quoted by Williams. Cotton, however, vigorously denied having a hand in this document in his 1647 response, *The Bloudy Tenent Washed and Made White in the Bloud of the Lamb*. In both cases, Cotton begins his rejoinder to Williams with a protest against the unauthorized appearance of his words.[13] Cotton states in his *Reply to Mr. Williams* that while he owns the letter to be his, "how it came to be put in print, I cannot imagine. Sure I am it was without my Privitie: and when I heard of it, it was to me unwelcome Newes, as knowing the truth, and weight of Plinies speech, 'Aliud est scribere uni, aliud omnibus.'"[14] Cotton suggests that "there be those who thinke it was published by Mr. Williams himselfe, or by some of his friends, [who] tooke more libertie than God alloweth, to draw forth a private admonition to publick notice in a disorderly way."[15] He initially suspected Sabine Staresmore, an associate of Williams's with Separatist leanings.[16]

The 1647 appearance of *The Bloudy Tenent Washed* was Cotton's first legitimate participation in this debate, and did not appear nearly four years elapsed. Williams, who faced the same challenges, retorted with *The Bloody Tenent yet more Bloody*, but not until 1652. Roger Williams enjoyed the last word, for Cotton died before he could respond.

The form of the debate becomes something like playing chess by mail, and given its desultory conclusion, it is hard to imagine a referee awarding a win to either antagonist. Beyond the content of debate, or its outcome, it is worth remembering that the entire exchange was one Cotton would have preferred not to have. However, Cotton's woes as an unwilling author are not limited to this antagonistic context. His lack of control over the texts appearing with his name is symptomatic of a challenge he faced throughout his years in New England. As the title of this chapter suggests, Cotton enjoyed authorial control over no more than half of the titles he published. Nor is this phenomenon unique to Cotton. Like Cotton, the other leading lights of the Bay Colony's ministers stayed in New England, and did not travel back, so Cotton's experience reflects the challenges New England's clergy faced in participating in the momentous political and religious debates of the 1640s. The ocean made the ideological work of orthodoxy harder, even as it made the political work of dissent easier.

II: Spinning Cotton

The half of Cotton's work where he lacks authorial control consists of three varieties, broadly speaking. There are unreliable transcriptions, untimely publications, and unauthorized publication. In this final category, one might include published responses to unfriendly queries. The kinds of distortions each can produce warrant separate description, for each has its own way of unraveling Cotton's authority and autonomy as an author. Of the thirty-six imprints with Cotton as the author that appeared between 1633, the year of his migration, and 1653, the year after his death, eighteen fall into one of the categories of compromised authorship. There are nine transcribed sermons, one untimely publication, three unauthorized letters, and five responses to queries.

First and most innocently, almost all of Cotton's sermons appearing after his emigration were prepared from the notes of others. Such publications were intended to honor Cotton, but they were transcribed from notes of varying reliability, and frequently many years after they were preached, and as such are difficult to accept as fully representative of Cotton's later thinking. While many important texts have been produced under such circumstances, such as Saussure's *Course in General Linguistics*, from the author's standpoint it is not ideal. One need only imagine the trepidation that might attend a professor opening a book prepared by his or her students from his or her lecture notes to grasp the difficulty Cotton faced.

These delays could also produce a second, more damaging distortion, when controversial works circulating in manuscript appeared in print after the publication of other texts representing a later stage of Cotton's thought. Continuing the analogy to academic life, a professor might well be dismayed if his or her seminar papers appeared in print after articles derived from those papers had already been published.

Third, and most harmful, was the deliberate publication of private correspondence of Cotton with the intent to discredit him—and a collateral phenomenon, which was the publication of his responses to unfriendly queries from London Presbyterians. Here, to conclude the analogy, it is hard to imagine who would welcome an unauthorized anthology of their email messages.

To consider the first case, while Cotton owes a considerable portion of his reputation to his published sermons and sermon series, such as *Gods promise to his plantations* (1634), *The powring out of the Seven Vials* (1642), and the *Exposition of the whole book of Canticles* (1642, 2nd ed. 1648) these sermons have two major liabilities as reflections of Cotton's thought. In many cases, they appeared in print decades after he preached them, and the texts were prepared from the notes of his auditors. In addition to these examples, there are other sermons that appeared posthumously, like the *Commentary on the first Epistle of John* (1656). Some, like *God's Promise,* appeared in a timely fashion, but most appeared after long intervals. As a rule, these sermons appear through the agency of one of Cotton's auditors, and without the minister's approval or participation. Apologies for this manner of transmission are formulaic in the prefaces to Cotton's sermons: in a preface to the *Way of Life* (1641) William Morton admits, "How gratefull it may be to this Reverend author, that this work of his should come abroad into the publick censure, I know not . . . I could have wished (if it might have been) that it had passed under his censure . . . but seeing it was designed for the Presse, that desire I had of the Publicke good and the respect I have ever owed the author, inclined me to lend it the best furtherance I could."[17] Introducing the *Seven Vials,* one I.H. (John Humfry) characterizes the text as "a taste of the ordinary week-dayes Exercise of that Reverend man, taken from his own mouth, whose Pen would have more fully answered thy greatest expectations, could his time, afforded him more liberty and leisure."[18] However, John Winthrop commented in his Journal that "Mr. Humfrey had gotten the notes from some who had took them by characters and printed them in London . . . which was a great wrong to Mr. Cotton . . . for it had been fit he should have perused and corrected the copy before it had been printed."[19]

Recognizing this irregularity does not erase Cotton's contributions as a theologian—indeed, the number of his sermons that were published from parishioners' notes is a tribute to his influence and charisma, while posthumous publication is a measure of the strength of his legacy. In the culture of revolutionary London, however, it does diminish his authority as an author. In an intensely contentious print culture, the way Cotton appeared in print often deprived him of a significant degree of control. Simply put, in an arena where replies, animadversions, remonstrances, apologies, and answers to the same question could appear on London bookstalls within days of one another, decade-old sermons lacked the polemical vigor that readers in revolutionary London had come to expect.[20]

Indeed, Cotton's removal to Boston may have promoted the appearance of these kinds of texts: Introducing *Gods Mercie Mixt with his Justice* (1641) Matthew Swallowe describes the text as "his mantle left behind him," namely "some broken notes of his powerfull soule searching sermons, taken from his mouth by the diligent hand of some well-disposed hearers and followers" (A2). While the appearance of these texts in the early 1640s is a testament to the enduring esteem of Cotton's London friends, the notion of imperfect transcripts of sermons delivered in relative youth to a provincial audience suddenly appearing in Revolutionary London, even as matters of faith and polity were the subject of passionate debate, seems to have made Cotton uneasy—Cotton complained in a 1648 sermon on the same text that his 1642 Brief Exposition of the whole Book of Canticles was published without his "privitie."[21]

Cotton's followers may have done him a disservice—diluting his authority by publishing belated and poorly transcribed sermons—but similar efforts on behalf of controversial works could have a more damaging result. The *Keys of the Kingdom of Heaven* (1644) Cotton regarded as his definitive statement of Congregational polity; its assertions were muddled by the subsequent appearance of the *Way of the Churches of New England* (1645), an earlier manuscript that had circulated in that form and that reached the press after Cotton's authorized pronouncements.

In the case of the *Keys* and the *Way*, the phenomenon of scribal publication complicates questions of publication and authorial agency. Building on Harold Love's influential study of scribal publication in seventeenth-century England, Philip Round argues that the circulation of texts in manuscript played a significant role in the cultural life of New England. To be sure, such influential texts as Bradford's and Winthrop's histories, and Bradstreet's poetry, circulated and were familiar in New England at the time of their composition, and well in advance of their belated publication. Manuscript letters, Round argues, "helped to extend the metropolitan discursive network that was beginning to unite Puritans into a formidable political community across England."[22]

"Discursive network" suggests a coherence and consensus that empirical evidence does not support. This "formidable political community," of course, faced vigorous opposition, and scribal publication facilitated the opposition to this community as much as it enabled its members to circulate their writings. In particular, the *Way of the Churches of Christ in New England* (1645) circulated in manuscript and attracted the disapprobation of the Presbyterian apologist Robert Baillie's *Dissuasive from the Errours of our Time*, before Cotton's supporters brought it to the press so that Cotton's argument might enjoy the same currency as Baillie's uncharitable rejoinder. In Cotton's thinking, however, the *Way of the Churches of New England* was an exercise preliminary to *The Keys of the Kingdom of Heaven*, and not intended for public view. It was left to John Owen, years later, to clarify that the *Way* had been printed "without the author's privity, and to his regret."[23]

The Atlantic magnified the difficulty and delay Cotton faced in debating his Presbyterian opponents by responding to this sort of unauthorized publication. In *The Way of the Congregational Churches Cleared* (1648) (distinct from *Way of the Churches of New England*), shepherded through the press by Nathaniel Holmes, Cotton responds to Daniel Cawdry's rejoinder to his *Keys of the Kingdom of Heaven*, *Vindicae Clavium* (1645). In *Vindicae Clavium*, Cawdry makes much of inconsistencies between Cotton's *Keys*, and his *Way of the Churches of New England*. In response, Cotton opens by pointing out, "I have not had liberty to peruse the *Way* since it was published: but I see by the first words of it that the publishers had not the copy which was taken hence from me, but an imperfect transcript. But I do believe what the publishers do report . . . there is no material difference between the *Key* and the *Way*." Here, Cotton must defend this text, which was published without his consent, of which he has not a copy, and to an audience with rather different concerns than those of three years previously. Quite simply, the time it took for manuscripts to cross, and for books to return, across the Atlantic makes it nearly impossible for Cotton to defend himself against his Presbyterian antagonists, and to be a full participant in the momentous debates of the 1640s.

The career of John Cotton offers a useful perspective on the distinct challenges and opportunities that shaped the portion of transatlantic discourse that originated in America. In considering the dissemination of his ideas in New England and Old as two very different contexts, we gain a new understanding of how these key articulations of the New England Way functioned on both sides of the Atlantic. The record suggests that effort of ministers and magistrates to control events, ideas, and discourse in New England was mirrored in their loss of control over the means, timing, and nature of their appearance in print in London.

In an intensely contentious and volatile print culture, several of the ways Cotton appears in print deprived him of a significant portion of control. Conversely, Roger Williams was able to represent himself and his colony's interests much more directly, though still through the medium of print. Williams's presence in London gave him an advantage in his battle with Cotton and the Bay Colony authorities. While Williams had the eyes and ears of Vane and Parliament, Cotton was forced to send his salvos from across the ocean, at targets that shifted and changed in the time it took for his words to reach England.

2. A KEY FOR THE GATE

Roger Williams, Parliament, & Providence

Among the first generation of English settlers in New England, Roger Williams is one of the most appealing figures for present-day readers. In contrast to contemporaries whose names are bywords for intolerance, scholars hail Williams as a prophet of tolerance; in contrast to neighbors who could imagine relations with Indians only in terms of killing them or converting them, scholars remember Williams for his efforts to understand the natives of America. Thus, a 1991 biography of Williams asserts that while he "had no hand in writing the First Amendment, [he] would have taken great pleasure in its guarantees."[1] In the context of Euro-Indian relations, the ethno-historian James Axtell contends that Williams knew the Indians "better than anyone else," and that he was among the first to suggest that "English had no monopoly on virtue" and even that Indians were "more Christian than Christians."[2]

These views of Williams as an advocate for native Americans and for religious liberty are supported by his two best-known works, *A Key into the Language of America*, an account of New England Indian language, and *The Bloudy Tenent*, a defense of religious freedom. However, simply identifying Williams as a herald of tolerance and understanding for later generations can obscure his achievement in his own time. Williams's contribution was not simply that he espoused tolerance of racial or religious difference, but that he created a geographical space where these principles could be put into action. Without an instrument of civil government for Providence Plantations, Williams's admirable opinions would have found no means of expression. In this light, the most important achievement in

Williams's career is not the *Bloudy Tenent* or the *Key*, but the patent he secured from Parliament for Providence Plantations in 1644.

Williams's London publications in 1643–44 are central to this effort. The grant of this instrument of government from Parliament was the product of Williams's time in revolutionary London, a mission framed by the publication of the *Key* in September 1643, shortly after his arrival, and the *Bloudy Tenent* in the summer of 1644, at the time of his departure. The Providence patent not only preserved the territory of Providence Plantations from a rival claim made by Thomas Weld and Hugh Peter on behalf of Massachusetts, but it also permitted the religious liberty and cultural toleration for which Williams is celebrated.

Through the texts he published during his 1643–44 stay in London, Williams forged connections between his troubles in New England and England's civil turmoil. In particular, Williams was able to use *A Key into the Language of America* to develop the radical revision of Anglo-Indian relations he used to defend his claim to a settlement on the shores of Narragansett Bay. More specifically, Roger Williams was able to secure a home for his millennial idealism by engaging with the intellectual trends that were then circulating in London among the overseers and underwriters of American colonies. Within the pansophic philosophy promulgated by Jan Amos Comenius and popular among Parliamentary leaders, Williams found a literary form he could use to revise English conceptions of Native Americans. Williams's claim to Providence rested on purchase from Narragansett sachems; the *Key* works to persuade the overseers of colonization in London that these savages are in fact civilized enough to own and sell land.

Ultimately, the texts that Williams published worked in concert to produce a vision of the new American world that could be echoed back to him by Parliament, in the form of an instrument of colonial authority. The patent is a condensed version of the texts Williams produced while in England, returned to him imbued with political power. In its religious latitude and its recognition of Native American land claims, the patent for Providence Plantations from Parliament authorizes Williams's dissenting view of America in both its racial and religious dimensions.

Understanding Williams's accomplishments has significance outside the narrow boundaries of the settlement he founded. Rereading Williams's early writings as part of an integrated political campaign to preserve Providence Plantations from the Bay Colony's territorial ambitions does more than simply clarify his efforts on behalf of his colony—it must change the way we read collateral documents from Massachusetts. Williams's success reminds us that his more orthodox neighbors in Massachusetts were never "left alone with America," but faced ongoing challenges to the polity, ecclesiology, and survival of their colony.[3] In particular, *New Englands First Fruits* (1643) appears much more apologetic and defensive in the context of the *Key*.

That this discursive sphere spans the Atlantic Ocean makes it harder to recognize, but no less important. The Atlantic has emerged as a popular rubric for scholars in recent years, and this heuristic has offered important insights into the history and culture of populations on both sides of the ocean. While the Atlantic links the disparate communities on its shores, the physical and temporal barrier this body of water posed shapes the discourse that circulated among far-flung members of the Atlantic world. Williams's success in London demonstrates the peculiar importance of the physical presence of the Atlantic Ocean in the middle of the Atlantic world. Writing from America for London presses and readers presents both challenges and opportunities for New England colonists. As the previous chapter details, John Cotton's absence from metropolitan London compromised his participation in the momentous debates of the 1640s. Conversely for Williams, a presence in person on one side of the Atlantic, and a presence in print on the other, were essential to his effort to serve both his colony and his conscience. At the same time, a crucial feature of his participation in London's print culture is his exploitation of the ability that a text has to be present when its author is absent.

I: The Removes of Roger Williams

Roger Williams's experience of the west shore of the Atlantic was a turbulent one. He arrived with his wife in Boston on 9 February 1630/1, part of the first wave of Puritan migration to New England.[4] After a brief sojourn there, he moved to Salem. Despite a distinguished intellectual reputation, he began to make enemies among the Boston ministers and magistrates and moved to Plymouth, but he returned to Salem in the fall of 1633. A variety of controversies with the Bay Colony authorities filled his time there, most notably one concerning a manuscript Williams wrote on Anglo-Indian relations that attacked the very premise of the English colonial project. The manuscript does not survive, but Massachusetts Bay Company Governor Winthrop's reaction to it indicates that Williams took issue with the prevalent English conviction that, as the American continent lay beyond the pale of Christendom, it was the prerogative of an English sovereign to grant swaths of it to his subjects with a stroke of the pen.[5]

The controversy between Williams and the Bay Colony soon made coexistence untenable for both parties. Unmoved by Thomas Hooker's admonitions to recant, Williams was banished from the Bay Colony by the General Court on 9 October 1635. Williams, who had taken ill before his trial, and whose wife had just delivered their second child, was granted a six-week stay of sentence, under the condition that he cease disseminating his blasphemous opinions. Evidently, Williams continued his objectionable activities anyway, and in January 1635/6, the Bay Colony ordered his immediate arrest and transportation to England, sending a representative to Salem to execute the sentence. Evidently warned of his impending arrest by John Winthrop, among others, Williams fled Salem, one step ahead of his would-be captors.

On 24 March 1637/8, Williams secured a deed for Providence from the Narragansett sachems, Miantonomo and Canonicus, stating that they had conveyed to him "the lands and meadowes, upon the two fresh rivers called Mooshawsuck and Wanassquatucket, doe now by these presents, establish and confirm the bounds of those lands, from the river and lands at Pautuckqut, the great hill of Notquonckanet, on the northwest, and the town of Maushapogue on the west."[6] On 27 July 1640, having previously apportioned the land he purchased among those who joined him on the shore of Narragansett Bay, Williams joined with his fellow settlers in drawing up a civil compact.[7] However, both Plymouth and Massachusetts coveted the Williams settlement and its port; some of Williams's neighbors wanted to compound with one of these more established governments sanctioned by England. In the face of mounting pressures on his settlement, both from within and without, Williams sailed for London in the early summer of 1643, in an effort to secure a warrant for his settlement from England's government. The port of Boston was closed to him, of course, and because Providence was then a port of little account, Williams was forced to journey overland to New Amsterdam to get passage.

He arrived in June 1643 to a London that was preoccupied with civil war and the Solemn League and Covenant, which was approved by Parliament on 25 September of that year. Williams published *A Key into the*

Language of America on 7 September 1643. His *Mister Cotton's Letter Examined* appeared on 5 February 1643/4, after the publication of a letter of Cotton's in late 1643. Turning to British affairs, Williams published *Queries of Highest Consideration* on 9 February 1643/4. Slightly more than a month later, Williams received a patent for Providence Plantations, on 14 March 1643/4. *The Bloudy Tenent of Persecution* appeared on 15 July 1644, not long before Williams must have left London, which was as just as well for him, as it was ordered burned by the public hangman on 9 August 1644. *Christenings Make Not Christians*, the final product of this trip, appeared early in 1645. By the time this work appeared to the London public, Williams had been back in America for several months. Winthrop notes in his journal that on 17 September 1644, Williams returned to America, able to land at Boston because of a letter of protection signed by several members of Parliament, including his old patron William Masham, as well as Cornelius Holland and Miles Corbet.[8]

Scholars have overlooked several curious features of the sequence, timing, and nature of Williams's activities in London. He published the most sustained articulation of his beliefs, *The Bloudy Tenent*, on the eve of his departure, and arranged to have the most controversial of his publications, *Christenings Make Not Christians*, appear once he was far from London. The publishing choices he made while in London are also curious. He revived two separate and long-forgotten disputes with John Cotton to retail to a London with plenty of current controversies clamoring for its attention. Williams could not have designed *Queries*, his most overtly political effort, to antagonize more readers if he had been trying to do so: It questioned not only the actions of the Westminster Assembly, but also the very validity of its existence, asking, "What warrant from the Lord Jesus for the Assembly of Divines?"[9]

Most curious, though, are the timing, form, and content of *A Key into the Language of America*. Williams came to England on an urgent political mission, and he also had an intense personal stake in the momentous issues of church and state that were being debated when he arrived. The rest of Williams's publications during this visit have immediate and apparent relevance to current political and religious affairs in England, with attendant ramifications for New England. However, before he published any of these documents, Williams produced a guide to the language of the Indians of New England, which one would imagine to be the work of a man of an inquisitive spirit, eager to produce a curiosity for what

William Wood called the "mind travelling reader," but one possessed of considerably more leisure than Williams himself enjoyed.[10]

Reconstructing Williams's activities and the motivations for them during his trip to London is critical to understanding how he was able to secure the patent for Providence Plantations. Unfortunately, all of Williams's correspondence is missing from 8 March 1640/1 to 25 June 1645, covering the entire trip to London and more than a year before and after.[11] To understand how Williams secured the patent, we must consider the relation between his surviving published work, and the ideas and interests of the intended audiences for his various publications.

The *Key* is the most puzzling production of Williams's trip to England. Leaving aside questions of timing and content for the moment, the best explanation for the form of the *Key* lies outside the parameters of the literature of American contact and exploration; as commentators have observed, it is unique in its form and concerns among the many accounts of North America and its indigenous people that issued forth from London presses in the first half of the seventeenth century. Williams was one of many colonists to supply English readers with Indian words, but he does not produce a dictionary or word list. As Laura Murray points out, Indian vocabularies were a common feature of early colonial texts, functioning as "authenticating and decorative devices"; she cites John Smith, William Strachey, and William Wood as examples.[12] Williams, however, offers not a list of words, but a carefully structured series of dialogues between English and Indians. As anomalous as the *Key* may appear in the context of colonial discourse, in another contemporary context it fits quite comfortably, for in its dialogic structure and linguistic focus, the *Key* is a close relative of the linguistic manuals that were a hallmark of the pansophist movement in the 1630s and 1640s. This movement, with Francis Bacon as its intellectual progenitor and the Czech philosopher Jan Amos Comenius as its standard-bearer, saw utopian promise in the possibility of universal knowledge and linguistic competence.

As the dearth of recent scholarship in English suggests, Comenius is not prominent in the minds of most intellectual historians of Revolutionary England. However, this Czech philosopher and educator enjoyed a good deal of esteem among many of the prominent members of the Parliamentary side, and his works circulated widely among English-speaking readers as well as in Europe. Comenius's *Janua Trilinguarum Reserata* (the gate of three languages opened) appeared in 1631 at Leszno, and in the same year, John Anchoran produced an English version; Adrian Johns numbers fifteen separate editions by various combinations of translators and printers appearing in England between 1630 and when Williams made his visit.[13] This *Janua* was inspired in its form by the 1615 *Janua Linguarum* of William Bathe, a Jesuit priest who intended his book as an aid to Jesuit missionaries in the Americas.[14] As Johns notes, one reason for the proliferation of editions of Comenius's book lay in the very form of the work, which was parallel translations of sentences in three or more languages; it was natural for enterprising translators to extend this project to embrace new languages. Comenius himself observed in retrospect: "It happened, as I could not have imagined possible, that that puerile little work was received with a sort of universal applause by the learned world." Comenius uses "puerile" in the sense of "juvenile," for he saw the *Janua* as an early stage of a larger educational project, which extended the structure of the *Janua* to encompass things as well as words. Barbara Lewalski, describing the Comenian scheme promoted in England by Samuel Hartlib and John Drury, explains: "In the Noble Schools boys from ages eight to thirteen would study the subjects of the common school, as well as *Januas* for Latin, Greek and Hebrew.'[15] Despite the disappointment of his grander ambitions for his English visit of 1641-2, Comenius does comment that the popularity of this book "was testified . . . by translations into the various popular tongues . . . all the European tongues, [and] such Asiatic tongues as the Arabic, the Turkish, the Persian, and even the Mongolian."[16]

Both the form of the work and the philosophy of its adherents suggested the reiteration of this form to embrace other tongues. Looking back, in his *Linguarum Methodus Novissima* (1649), Comenius hoped that his *Janua* would surpass Bathe's in its ability to help travelers to America learn native languages and teach the natives English or Latin.[17] Given Williams's interest in appealing to the same Parliamentary leaders who had invited Comenius to England little more than a year before Williams arrived, it is no accident that the title of Williams's work evokes the language of doors opening. At least one reader has previously noted the similarities between the *Key* and these popular linguistic materials, pointing out that "Williams's pedagogical thinking . . . suggests acquaintance with the most progressive contemporary thinking about the teaching of foreign languages, such as that promoted by Jan Comenius in his *Janua Linguarum*."[18] Anne Myles observes that Williams and Comenius share an approach of teaching language through "text that discourses in simple terms on the names of things," but she notes this affinity between the *Janua* and the *Key* as an indication of Williams's intellectual sophistication. The *Key* does indicate Williams's awareness of current intellectual trends, but this awareness also has political dimensions that are critical for Williams's errand to London.

In *The Intellectual Origins of the English Revolution Revisited*, Christopher Hill lists the supporters of Comenius and his work in the 1630s and 1640s, observing, "It is very nearly a list of members of the Providence Island Company. It is a list of the leaders of the opposition in the Long Parliament."[19] It also evolves out of the nexus of Revolutionary leadership Robert Brenner describes as the "aristocratic colonizing opposition."[20] Of more immediate concern to Williams is that the Committee for Foreign Plantations, the body charged by Parliament to regulate colonial affairs, mirrors the composition of the Comenians and the Providence Island Company. In essence, the members of Parliament charged with weighing Williams's suit were the same members who brought Comenius to England in 1641–42. As R. F. Young explains in his account of Comenius's visit to England in 1641–42, "Comenius genuinely believed that he had been invited by Parliament, but the available evidence suggests that Samuel Hartlib had summoned him on behalf of . . . Lord Mandeville, Pym, Lord Brooke and others." These men were all members of the Committee for Foreign Plantations, which would review Williams's suit in 1644; the summons Comenius thought was an official invitation was in fact part of a sermon preached to Parliament on 29 November 1640 by John Gauden, entitled *The Love of Truth and Peace* (printed by order of Parliament in early 1641) to entreat Comenius. Gauden was later the Bishop of Exeter and of Worcester, but at this time, he was vicar of Chippenham and chaplain to Robert Rich, Earl of Warwick, who three years later would become the head of the Committee for Foreign Plantations.[21] In the patent it bestowed on Williams, the Committee for Foreign Plantations was explicit in its praise for Williams's "printed Indian labours," leaving no doubt that it was a receptive audience for the *Key*. The knowledge we have of the colonial political interests and pansophic intellectual pursuits of this body allows us to understand Williams's text as that of a colonial appeal to metropolitan authority that encompasses both the between the pragmatic and ideological concerns of his mission. At the same time, Williams shapes the form of his text to appeal to his powerful audience.

When the ideas of Comenius have been associated with New England, it has generally been in one of two misleading ways. In "Comenius and the Indians of New England," Robert Young suggests that Comenius supporters in Parliament thought "Comenius's scheme . . . might in some

XIII. De Animalibus, & primò de Avibus.	**XIII.** Of living creatures, and firſt of Birds.	**XIII.** Des Animaux, & premierement des Oiſeaux
135 Qvicquid vita, ſenſu, & motu præditum eſt, animal eſt.	135 Whatſoever hath life feeling oʒ ſenſe and motion, is a living Creature.	135 Tout ce qui a vie, ſentiment & mouvement, eſt un Animal.
136 Alites enim volant: Aquatilia natant (illæ pennis, hæc pinnis) quadrupedia currunt, Reptilia repunt.	136 Foʒ winged fowles fly: they that live in water ſwim (thoſe with feathers, theſe with finnes) the foure-footed run oʒ goe, creeping things doe creepe.	136 Car les Oyſeaux volent, les Aquatiques ou qui vivent en l'eau, nagent; (ceux-là avec des plumes, ceux-cy avec des nageoires) les beſtes a quatre pieds courent; les Reptiles rampent ou ſe trainent.
137 Volucres ſunt bipedes, (Manucodiatam eſſe apodem dicunt) & plumatæ, & roſtratæ: excepto Veſpertilione, qui & piloſus & dentatus eſt.	137 Birds oʒ fowles have two feete, (men ſay that Manucodiata hath none) and are feathered, and have bills oʒ beakes, except the Reremouſe, oʒ Bat, which is hairy and toothed.	137 Les Volailles ont deux pieds, (on dit que la Manuque n'en a point) & des plumes, & un bec; hormis la Chauve-ſouris, qui a du poile & des dents.
138 Roſtro colligentes grana ingluviem refarciunt, nulla mingit.	138 Gathering graine with their beakes, they fill the cram oʒ crop, none doth piſſe.	138 Cueillants les graines avec leur bec, ils en rempliſſent leur poche; nul ne piſſe.
139 Procreationis cauſa nidos ſtruunt: (Halcyon in ipſo pelago.)	139 Foʒ procreation ſake they build up neſts (the Halcyon on the very Sea.)	139 Ils baſtiſſent leurs nids pour procreation, (Halcyon dans la Mer meſme.
140 Tum pariunt ova (quæ ſub teſta albumen, & vitellum ſeu luteum occultant) iiſque incubantes pullos excludunt.	140 Afterwards they bʒing foʒth (oʒ breed) egges (which hid under the ſhell, the white and the yoalke) and lying thereon. hatch their young ones.	140 Puis ils y ponnent (ou font) des Oeufs, (qui cachent ſoubs la coque, la glaire & le rouge ou moyeu) & s'y couchant deſſus, eſcloſent leurs poulcins.
141 Rapaces ſunt Vultur, Milvus, Accipiter, Falco, Niſus; quæ unguibus uncis Turtures dilaniant.	141 Ravening foules are the Vulture, the Gryppe, the Kite, the Saker, the Hauke, the Eagle, the Faulcon, the Hobby, the Oſpʒay, which with their crooked clawes, teare and rent Turtle doves.	141 Les Oyſeaux raviſſans ſont, le Vautour, le Milan, l'Eſprevier, le Faulcon, l'Aigle, qui deſmembrent les Tourterelles de leur griffes crochues.
142 Noctua noctu cernit, interdiu cæcutit: ut & aliæ nocturnæ, Bubo, Aſio, Scops, Aluco, Vſula, Strix, Caprimulgus.	142 An Owle ſees in the night, and waxeth blind in the day time, as alſo other night-birds, an Owle, Aſio, a Scrick-Owle, a Horne, Scops, the Owlet, a Milker of Goats.	142 Le chathuant void de nuict, & eſt aveugle de jour, comme auſſi les autres oyſeaux nocturnes, le Hibou, le Scinre, le Limare, la Chevecoe, la Freſay, la Tette-chevre.
143 Phaſiani, Otides, (Tardæ) Tetraones (Vrogalli) Malea, Grides (Gallopavones) Capones, Attagenes, Perdices, Coturnices, in deliciis habentur.	143 Pheſants, Buſtards oʒ Horne-Owles, Biſtards, French Peacockes, Capons, Morhens, Godwits, Partridges, Quailes, are held foʒ delicious and dainty meat.	143 Les Phaiſans, les Outardes, les Tetaons, les Paons maſl s, les Chapons, les Francolines, les Perdrix, les Cailles, ſont tenus pour viandes delicieuſes.
144 Olor (Cygnus) Fulica, Mergus, Querquedula,	144 The Swan, the Fen-ducke, a Didopper, a Coʒmoʒant, oʒ a Gull, a	144 Le Cygne, la Foulque, le Plongeon, la Cercerelle, le Cor- Onocratalos.

140 Tum

FIGURE 3: From Jan Amos Comenius, *The Gate of Tongues Unlocked and Opened* (London: 1637). *Courtesy of Houghton Library, Harvard College Library STC 15080.*

Oyle good for many uses, but especially for their annoynting of their heads. And of the chips of the Walnut-Tree (the barke taken off) some *English* in the Countrey make excellent Beere both for Taft, strength, colour, and in offensive opening operation:

Safaunckapâmuck.	*The Saffafrasse Tree.*
Mifhquâwtuck.	*The Cedar tree.*
Côwaw-éfuck.	*Pine-young Pine.*
Wenomesíppaguafh.	*The Vine-Tree.*
Micúckaskeete.	*A Medow.*
Tataggoskituafh.	*A fresh Medow.*
Maskituafh.	*Grasse or Hay.*
Wékinafh-quafh.	*Reed, Reedes.*
Manisímmin.	*To cut or mow.*
Quffuckomineânug.	*The Cherry Tree.*
Wuttáhimneafh.	*Strawberries.*

Obf. This Berry is the wonder of all the Fruits growing naturally in those parts: It is of it selfe Excellent: so that one of the chiefest Doctors of *England* was wont to say, that God could have made, but God never did make a better Berry: In some parts where the *Natives* have planted, I have many times seen as many as would filla good ship within few miles compasse: the *Indians* bruise them in a Morter, and mixe them with meale and make Strawberry bread.

Wuchipoquáme

Wuchipoquáme-neafh.	*A kind of sharp Fruit like a Barbary in taft.*

Saseminéafh another sharp cooling Fruit growing in fresh Waters all the Winter, Excellent in conferve againft Feavers.

Wenómeneafh.	*Grapes.*
Wuttahimnasíppa-guafh.	*Strawberry leaves.*
Pefhaûjuafh.	*Violet leaves.*
Nummoúwinneem.	*I goe to gather.*
Mowinne-aûog.	*He or they gather.*
Atáuntowafh.	*Clime the Tree.*
Ntáuntawem.	*I clime.*
Punnoûwafh.	*Come downe.*
Npunnowaûmen.	*I come downe.*
Attitaafh.	*Hurtle-berries.*

Of which there are divers sorts sweete like Currants, some opening, some of a binding nature.

Saûtaafh are these Currants dried by the *Natives*, and so preserved all the yeare, which they beat to powder, and mingle it with their parcht meale, and make a delicate dish which they cal *Saûtáuthig*; which is as sweet to them as plum or spice cake to the *English.*

They also make great use of their Strawberries having such abundance of them, making Strawberry bread, and having no other

H   Food

FIGURE 4: From Roger Williams,
A Key into the Language of America (London: 1643).
*Courtesy of Houghton Library, Harvard College Library *EC P1483 645hg.*

way be associated with the missionary and educational work among the natives in New England."[22]

In later years, once Puritan missionary to the Indians John Eliot and his associates were active, this connection makes sense: The name of a Native American student, Joel Jacomis, dated 1665, was inscribed in a copy of Comenius's *Janua Aurea Linguarum*. A copy of Anchoran's pirated translation of the *Janua* (1631) was among the volumes John Harvard willed to Harvard College in 1638.[23] However, at the time of Comenius's visit in 1641–42 and still at the time of Williams's trip to England in 1643–44, there was little missionary activity to celebrate. Indeed, *New Englands First Fruits* (1643) is an apology for the slow progress of the Bay Colony on this front in light of Williams's progress demonstrated in the *Key*: "wonder not that wee mention no more instances at present: but consider, first, their infinite distance from Christianity."[24] Whatever the actual degree of interest Comenius took in the souls of Native Americans, his supporters would be hard pressed to congratulate the orthodox New England colonies for their work in that area up to 1643, when Williams was seeking protection from these same colonies.

The other common association between Comenius and New England is a tradition that he was offered the presidency of Harvard College in the 1640s, but declined, going to Stockholm instead.[25] Will Monroe demonstrates several reasons why this story is improbable, but the tradition has persisted despite the evidence against it.[26] These associations, despite their traditional rather than factual basis, have the tendency to orient any interest in the American context of Comenius to orthodox institutions and people, and away from a less orthodox adaptation of his work, such as *A Key into the Language of America*. However, the model of the *Janua* is essential to Williams's appeal to Parliamentary leaders.

II: "Printed Indian Labours": The Work of The Key

Rendered in this familiar form, the *Key* works to construct Williams's version of America in the minds of his English readers, displacing a more traditional ideology of conquest and conversion. For Williams's claim to the Narragansett region by virtue of Indian purchase to have any validity, his radical notion that Native Americans could and did possess land would have to find traction in the minds of Englishmen.[27] Despite its didactic structure, the goal of the *Key* was not so much to teach Londoners how to speak to Americans, but rather to teach them how to think about America.

Despite taking the unassuming form of a linguistic and anthropological work, the *Key* is a tremendously subversive document. The most radical aspect of Williams's Indian lexicon is its title: "A Key into The Language of America: or an help to the language of the Natives in that part of America, called New-England." Specifically, the title asserts that the "Language of America" is the language of its natives, rather than any of the languages of European conquerors; Myra Jehlen observes that "its anomaly lies in the implication that Indians are human beings with whom it is important to speak."[28] Williams's equation naturally underscores the connection between the continent and its original inhabitants and asserts the unconventional notion that the Narragansett and their neighbors were autonomous peoples, like the English, Dutch, or Swedes, who were able to make and assert land claims. Indeed, the rhetorical construction of a civil American Indian society is one of the central goals of the *Key*. In asserting a right to the lands of Providence Plantations based on a sale by an Indian deed, rather than by royal fiat, Williams inverts the traditional process of colonial settlement. Thus, Williams must present the Narragansett as competent to convey and alienate land if his claim to the Narragansett Bay is to have any merit. For Williams, his pragmatic concerns resonate with his religious convictions: Because his millennial beliefs lead him to denounce the idea of "Christendom," the civility of his Native American neighbors is not contingent on their Christianity.

The form of this text is well suited to this task. Each chapter of the *Key* is broken up into vocabulary, social and cultural observations, and a poem, almost always with a didactic religious theme. Through the vocabulary, the prose observations, and the religious verse, Williams offers his London readers a pervasive sense of the humanity of the Narragansett Indians. Each section affords Williams a different kind of rhetorical opportunity.

For many scholars, especially those of a literary orientation, the principal interest of the *Key* lies in the poetic sections. Ivy Schweitzer, for example, devotes a chapter to the *Key* in her study of the "Lyric Poetry of Colonial New England."[29] This focus on Williams as a poet may be motivated in part by the paucity of verse productions among the sermons and tracts of seventeenth-century New England; however, Williams did not return to this form, and on the strength of the poetic sections of the *Key*, it is hard for even the most charitable reader to regard him as a rival of

Anne Bradstreet or Edward Taylor. In their critical edition of the *Key*, Teunessen and Hinz stress the importance of an integrated reading of each chapter, in order to recover the work's similarity to emblem books. Williams scholars owe a debt to Teunessen and Hinz for their editorial work, but their claim of the affinity of this text with medieval emblem books is not entirely persuasive, resting as it does on an assertion that Williams's dialogues replace the pictures (emblems) that are the central feature of emblem books. Instead, the different genres contained within the *Key* each work on the imagination of the reader in a distinct manner.[30]

If Williams's poetry has attracted the most scholarly attention, by the same token it is the dialogues that appear to be the most inert and normative aspect of this text; however, these "implicite dialogues" are central to the end Williams intended for his little book. In the account of the form he chooses for teaching the language in his "Directions for the use of the Language," Williams allows "A dictionary or Grammer Way I had consideration of, but purposely avoided, as not so accommodate to the Benefit of all, as I hope this Forme is." Williams continues, explaining that "A Dialogue also I had thoughts of but avoided for brevities sake, and yet (with no small paines) I have so framed every Chapter of it, as I may call it an Implicite Dialogue."[31] If anything, the layout seems to privilege Narragansett, by having the flow be from Narragansett into English, in contrast to John Eliot's translation of the Bible from English into Algonkian. However, the salient feature of this lexicon is its bilateral quality. "Translate" etymologically means "to carry across." Eliot's translation, for instance, carries the Gospel across to the Indians, but finds nothing in their language worth carrying back. Jehlen comments that Eliot's works are "true to the purpose of the catechism, which is to repeat verbatim what one has been taught."[32] The *Key*, by comparison, can be used to open the door from either side. In this context, the *Key* reads like a document that is an artifact of a transcultural "contact zone," while Eliot's Bible is an instrument deployed by Massachusetts to Christianize and thus regulate the Indian frontier.[33]

Williams's notion of an implicit dialogue helps us understand how English readers would read the linguistic portions of the *Key*. The dialogue runs both horizontally (translating) and vertically (conversing) on each page of text. If they read across in one direction or the other, readers can translate the language of England into the language of America or vice versa. The nature of text, however, implies another dialogue as well, one that runs down each column of the linguistic sections of the

Key. Then or now, it would require an extraordinarily patient reader to sound out each Indian phrase before translating it. Thus, the tendency for readers in London would be to let their eyes run down the column in their native tongue. It is no accident, in this context, that these phrases are commonly arranged in what reads like a dialogue if one reads down the English column. The reader, reading to himself or herself, imagines a dialogue between Indians and English, with the two speaking on equal terms. This effect is enhanced by the reader's awareness that a parallel conversation is happening in the other language in the adjacent column. This excerpt from the first chapter, "Of Salutation," indicates the effect that recurs throughout the text.

Literally as well as figuratively, the Londoner and the Narragansett are on the same page, just as the Moravian, Roman, and Turk can share the pages of the same *Janua*.[34]

The form of the dialogue also allows Williams to conjure two characters—the English speaker of Narragansett, and the Narragansett writer of English. As the illustration shows, the original text provides elaborate diacritical guides to pronunciation. If the Indian vocabulary was simply "decorative," to use Murray's term, Williams might not bother with the painstaking marks he includes as a guide to pronouncing the Narragansett words.[35] In his "Directions for the use of the language," Williams asserts that "Because the life of all languages is in the Pronuntiation, I have been at the paines and charges to Cause the Accents, Tones or sounds to be affixed." Williams specifically mentions the "Acutes, Graves, Circumflexes" he has included, and offers several examples of their importance, such as, "in "the word *Ewò He:* the sound or tone must not be put on *E,* but *wò* where the grave Accent is."[36]

Simultaneously, Williams bestows the gift of writing on a people who typically are represented as resorting to pictograms to represent their signatures on deeds. Lack of a written language was persistently invoked by European observers as evidence of the uncivilized state of Indians. As Gordon Sayre details, generations of European ethnographers worked hard not to recognize Indian systems of graphic communication as legitimate writing. As Rousseau summarized this view from a later perspective: "the depicting of objects is appropriate to a savage people; signs of words and propositions to a barbaric people, and the alphabet to civilized peoples."[37] In this context, the silent transcription of a spoken Indian language into Roman characters undergirds Williams's construction of the civil Indian interlocutor.

2   Of *Salutation.*

What cheare Nétop ? *is the generall salutation
of all Englib toward them,* Nétop *is friend.*

Netompaüog	*Friends.*

They are exceedingly delighted with Salutations in their own Language.

Neèn, Keèn, Ewò,	*I, you, he.*
Keén ka neen	*You and I.*
Asco wequássin	
Asco wequassunnúm- mis	*Good morrow.*
Askuttaaquompsìn ?	*How doe you ?*
Asnpaumpmaúntam	*I am very well.*
Taubot paump maúntaman	*I am glad you are well.*
Cowaúnckamish	*My service to you.*

Obſervation.

This word upon ſpeciall Salutations they uſe, and upon ſome offence conceived by the *Sachim* or Prince againſt any : I have ſeen the party reverently doe obeyſance , by ſtroking the Prince upon both his ſholders, and uſing this word,

Cowaúnckamish & Cuckquénamish	*I pray your favour.*
Cowaúnkamuck	*He ſalutes you.*
Aſpaumpmaúntam ſachim	*How doth the Prince ?*

          Aſpaum-

FIGURE 5: From Roger Williams,
A Key into the Language of America (London: 1643).

Beyond these implicit dialogues, the didactic options rejected by Williams also help clarify the political work of the text. Williams allows that he had considered presenting this material in "a dictionary or grammer way," but rejected that option in favor of this dialogue-driven model. As a result, if one were to imagine this text in terms of contemporary approaches to language teaching, the *Key* is more like a phrase book for tourists than a comprehensive textbook that provides a grammar and vocabulary as building blocks that allow the student to communicate in a given language. The chapters of the *Key* correspond to given situations, edify the reader concerning Indian culture, and provide appropriate phrases for "Salutation . . . Travell . . . Sports and Gaming," and so on. However, constructing phrases for situations not in the book from what Williams provides the reader would be tedious and haphazard, if not impossible. Williams rejects a "dictionary or grammer way" as "not so accommodate for the benefit of all," but in fact it is his own purposes that would not be suited by a lexicon or grammar of this Indian language. As anyone who has attempted to communicate in a foreign language with only a tourist phrase book can attest, the phrases one would like to have are rarely present in the phrase book, so the traveler is forced into the role of a reluctant actor in a series of scripts prepared by the author of the phrase book. By providing prescribed phrases for prescribed situations, Williams deliberately shapes the character of the discourse that can occur with the Indians in New England, or about them in England; the phrases Williams provides are for the traveler or trader, not for the soldier or evangelist. Substituting conversation for catechism, Williams regulates the application of English language to foreign subjects by teaching English subjects a foreign language.

The dialogues allow English readers to imagine a conversation with these far-off, fascinating people, while Williams's proto-anthropological observations give them an image of their interlocutors as members of a civil, humane, and well-regulated society. Later in the first chapter on salutation, Williams directs the reader: "From these courteous Salutations Observe in generall: There is a savour of civility and courtesie even amongst these wild Americans both amongst themselves and towards strangers."[38]

This representation of the civil Indian is at odds with the prevailing impressions furnished from New England, the most contemporary being *New Englands First Fruits*, which was published in early 1643. Describing the task of converting the Indians, the main obstacle is the aforementioned "infinite distance from Christianity," the reason for which is their "never having never been prepared there unto by any civility at all."[39] In a colonial context, one dramatic consequence of Williams's faith is the divorce of Christianity and civility: If Christianity and civility are not coextensive, it is possible to be civil without being Christian.

In the ensuing chapters of the *Key*, Williams extends this notion by constructing a view of a civil Indian society, with the requisite appurtenances of any such society. Williams labors to construct an image of Narragansett society that is in many respects like London: "They are of two sorts, (as the English are) rude and clownish . . . or sober and grave." This universalizing impulse permeates the text: "their Desire of, and delight in newes, is great, as the Athenians, and all men."[40] With his language, Williams seeks to narrow the difference between the English and the Narragansetts, observing, "Nature knowes no difference between Europe and Americans in blood, birth, bodies . . . God having of one blood made all mankind, Acts 17, and all by nature being children of wrath, Ephes 2."[41]

There are few moments in this text when Williams does not avail himself of the chance to offer evidence of the probity, civility, and general uprightness of his Narragansett neighbors. Describing Indian timekeeping, Williams comments, "They are punctuall in their promises of keeping time, and sometimes have charged mee with a lye for not punctually keeping time, though hindred."[42] On larger moral issues, in place of Thomas Morton's salty images of "lasses in beaver coats," Williams observes, "Their Virgins are distinguished by a bashfull falling downe of haire over their eyes."[43] Ultimately, the sense of their rectitude that Williams conveys integrates them into the reader's imagination as civil beings, not savage creatures. In Williams's account of their "coyne" not only does Williams use an English word for money to describe it, rather than peage, or wampum, but his translations also serve to establish a rate of exchange back and forth between Indian shell money and English pence and shillings.

Having rhetorically clothed these Indians with the civil virtues of punctuality, modesty, and economy, along with many other virtues, Williams can more easily assert what is for him perhaps the most important aspect of the *Key*. In "Of the Earth and the fruits thereof," Williams's first observation is that "The Natives are very exact and punctuall, in the bounds of their Lands, belonging to this or that Prince or People . . . . And I have knowne them to make bargaine and sale amongst themselves for a small piece, or quantity of ground." Maintaining an objective distance, Williams does not refer here to his own purchase, but explicitly challenges the familiar notion of *vacuum domicilium* articulated by Winthrop from the deck of the *Arabella*, and defended by Cotton: "notwithstanding a sinfull opinion amongst many that Christians have right to Heathens lands: but of the delusion of that I have spoke in a discourse concerning the Indians conversion."[44] This pamphlet, *Christenings Make Not Christians*, did not in fact appear until 1645, after Williams was back in Providence; at this stage, what is most notable about this gesture is that Williams deliberately suppresses his views on evangelizing Indians while he presses his suit to Parliament.

Considering his pessimism on the subject, it is no wonder that Williams prevented his views on the likelihood of converting the Indians from reaching London readers until he was back home with his patent. Indeed, *Christenings Make Not Christians* offers an expansion of the millennial concerns that become increasingly prevalent in the concluding poems of each chapter of the *Key*. Initially, these poems work to humanize the Indians by portraying the inhumanity of their Puritan neighbors:

> If natures sons both wild and tame,
> Humane and Courteous be:
> How ill becomes the Sonnes of God
> To want Humanity?[45]

However, as the *Key* progresses, this moral calculus gives way to a sense of the equal wretchedness of Indian and Englishman before the coming Judgment:

> How many millions now alive,
> Within few yeeres shall rot?
> O Blest that soule whose portion is,
> That Rock that changeth not.[46]

This millennial rhetoric becomes increasingly strident in the poetry toward the end of the *Key*. The final two stanzas explicate the nature of the coming Judgment:

> Two Worlds of men shall rise and stand
> 'Fore Christs most dreadfull barre;
> Indians, and English naked too
> That now most gallant are
> True Christ most glorious then shall make
> New Earth and Heavens New

> False Christs, false Christians then shall quake,
> O blessed then the True.[47]

More than manners, customs, or civility, the coming wrath of God renders worldly distinctions between English subject and savage Indian insignificant.

In presenting this work to the readers who would decide the fate of his colony, Williams legitimates himself as the proprietor of a plantation he has acquired through a civil transaction with a civil people. By inscribing the Narragansett Indians within a Comenian linguistic framework, Williams creates an American extension of the European *Janua*. Through this gate, Williams finds a route to connect his political aims with the intellectual interests of the Parliamentary overseers of colonization. His "printed Indian Labours," as the Committee for Foreign Plantations called them, secured the political autonomy of Providence.

III: Authorizing Providence

When he returned to America, Williams's credit with Parliament stood high. Landing at Boston, Williams was able to show Bay Colony authorities a letter of safe passage through the colony from which they had banished him, in addition to the patent. Addressed to the "Right Worshipful the Governour and Assistants . . . in the Plantation of Massachusetts Bay, in New England," the letter informed this body that "Having taken notice, some of us long time, of Mr. Roger Williams his good affections and conscience, and of his sufferings by our common enemies, the prelates . . . ."[48] This description of Williams's sufferings is curious, because the bulk of his travails had occurred in New England, far from Laud or his henchmen, so the Parliamentary signers of this letter seem to have intended this description as a call to solidarity against a common foe, or as a tacit reproof of the suffering Williams did actually endure at the hands of this reformed polity in Massachusetts.

The letter continues, explaining that in addition to his sufferings, Parliament has taken note of "his great industry and travail in his printed Indian Labours, the like whereof we have not seen extant from any part of America."[49] Indeed, these "printed Indian Labours" are cited as "in which respect it hath pleased both houses of Parliament to grant unto him and his friends with him a free and absolute charter of civil government for those parts of his abode."[50] Thus described, the nature and the scope of the document ratify Providence as "his abode," rebuffing the claims advanced by Weld and Peter; moreover, the patent is for "civil government," and makes absolutely no stipulations about religion. In the patent, if not in England at large, Williams's cries against state religion were heeded.

The letter to the Governor of the Bay Colony concludes with reference to the contentions in New England and expresses regret that "amongst good men, driven to the ends of the world, exercised with the trialls of a wilderness . . . there should be such a distance; we thought it fit . . . to express our great desires of both your utmost endeavours of nearer closing and of ready expressing of those good affections . . . in the actual performance of all your friendly offices."[51] In an immediate context, this warrants the passage of Roger Williams home to Providence; in a larger sense, the humiliating implication for Massachusetts is that the government of Providence Plantations is on an equal footing with its own.

The patent makes this legitimacy explicit. After a preamble detailing the Committee for Foreign Plantations' authority in this matter, the patent begins with an act of translation:

> And whereas there is a tract of land in the Continent of America aforesaid, called by the name of Narragansetts Bay Bordering North and North East on the Pattent of the Massachusetts East and South East on Plymouth Pattent South on the Ocean and on the West and North West Inhabited by Indians Called Nahigganzuks alias Narragansetts.[52]

With these words, Parliament translates Williams's Indian purchases of "the lands and meadowes, upon the two fresh rivers called Mooshawsuck and Wanassquatucket" into English law. Against the natural landmarks of the Indian deed, Providence is inscribed into an English colonial juridiscape, between the patents for Massachusetts and Plymouth. Also, the ongoing presence and property of the Narragansetts are acknowledged, possibly for the first time in English law, and in any event, this represents a different conception of native property rights than the "tracte of lande . . . not then actualie possessed by any other Christian Prince or State" of the Massachusetts charter of only fifteen years previous.[53]

The next "whereas" (the word introducing each warrant for the patent) details Williams's peculiar engagement with the Indians: "whereas divers well affected and industrious English inhabitants of the Townes of Providence, Portsmouth and Newport . . . have adventured to make a neerer neighborhood and sociaty with that great body of Narragansetts which may in time by the blessing of God upon theire endeavours Lay a surer foundation of happiness to all America."[54] The "neerer neighborhood and sociaty" commended by the patent conforms to the cultural exchange Williams describes in the *Key*; the "endeavours" are not evangelical, but instead the "blessing of God" may allow Anglo–Indian amity to advance the welfare of all in America. The absence of any evangelical charge is striking, considering the Bay Colony's recently resurgent interest in the field, not to mention that its charter stipulated that the "People were to be so governed as to win the natives to the Christian faith, which is the principal end of the plantation.[55]

These same Providence inhabitants, the patent explains, "have purchased, and are purchasing of and amongst the said Natives some other places, which may be convenient both for Plantations, and also for the Building of Ships."[56] Parliament not only legitimates Williams's purchases from Indians, but also empowers his fellows to make more.

The final premise for the patent acknowledges Williams's suit explicitly, and alludes to the Weld–Peter suit:

> And whereas the said English have represented their desire to the said Earle and commissioners to have theire hopefull beginnings aprooved and confirmed, by granteing unto them a free charter of civill incorporation and Government that they may order and governe themselves in such manner as to maintaine Justice and peace both amongst themselves and towards all men with whome they shall have to doe.[57]

"All men with whome they have to doe" would mean mostly Plymouth and Massachusetts; given the hostility that still existed toward their "hopefull beginnings," it certainly behooved Providence Plantations to have a sanction to "maintaine justice." Also worth noting is the latitude in the government, which Parliament "doe give, grant and confirme to the aforesaid Inhabitants," detailed as "full power and authoritie to govern and rule themselves . . . by such a form of civil government as by voluntary consent of all or the greatest part of them shall be found most suitable to theire estates and conditions."[58]

Unlike a charter drawn up for a colony not yet extant, Providence had an indigenous frame of government already in place. Thus, on the one hand, there was not the same need to delineate the administration of power. On the other hand, "voluntary consent of all or the greatest part of them" is a broad franchise for 1644, and the government so warranted had announced, in one of its first actions: "Wee agree, as formerly hath bin the liberties of the town, so still, to hould forth liberty of Conscience."[59] Williams's flight through the wilderness, the principles for which he was forced to flee, and his refuge among the Narragansetts are legitimated with "A free and absolute Charter of Civill incorporation to be knowne by the name of the Incorporacion of Providence Plantacions in the Narragansetts Bay in New England."[60] In its confirmation of an Indian land transfer, and its guarantee of liberty of conscience, the patent echoes the arguments Williams made in London, distilled into a form he can carry with him back to America.

Williams had to be patient, but he ultimately secured political sanction for the observance of his religious principles. This physical space on the shore of Narragansett Bay became the ground from which further religious dissent could be articulated. The *Key* and the other documents Williams published constitute an unwieldy medium of appeal, but they worked. Williams's dissenting message did not reform church and state in England, but Parliament did give him the opportunity to implement his reforms in America. In the context of colonial New England, Williams's achievement was to open up an alternate channel of transatlantic discourse—a way for dissidents to appeal from the colonies to London. Writing from the ground Williams secured, his neighbors would make further contributions to this new print culture of colonial dissent.

3. "A BELCHER-OUT OF ERROURS"

Samuel Gorton and the Atlantic Subject

Roger Williams demonstrated to his neighbors at home in Rhode Island that it was possible for a member of a religious minority to describe the state of affairs in New England in a way that would persuade Parliament to intervene on its behalf against Massachusetts. However, Williams's campaign for political autonomy and religious latitude involved disparate publications on several themes, rather than a single and explicit statement of his grievances. Samuel Gorton follows Williams's model in prosecuting a successful campaign against the persecutions of Massachusetts in London, but he refines Williams's practice by integrating a defense of his religious liberty, and representation of his Indian neighbors, into a single text that states his case against the Bay Colony.

To say that Gorton synthesizes the disparate elements of Williams's dissent is not to make a claim that Gorton possessed a concise or accessible prose style. He did not. Indeed, Gorton's enemies attacked his style as much as his ideas, a position he caricatures with the phrase "a Belcher-out of errours." The remark comes retrospectively, in Samuel Gorton's reply to an unflattering portrayal of him in Nathaniel Morton's *New Englands Memorial* (1669). Gorton, according to Morton, was a "sordid man," a "proud and pestilent seducer," given to infecting his neighbors with "familisticall allegories."[1] In a long letter in reply, Gorton asserts, "And however you term me a Belcher-out of errours, I would have you know that I hold my call to preach not inferiour to the call of any minister in this country."[2] In his account of the progress of New England, Morton assigns Gorton a bit part as a minor annoyance, especially when compared to struggles with Indians and Antinomians, and this dismissiveness has been the general approach of New England historians both then and now. Gorton, however, was one of the first New Englanders to use London presses to influence events in America, and to oppose entrenched Massachusetts ministers and magistrates successfully. Despite assertions of his insignificance from his opponents, Gorton's career demonstrates that through the medium of print, even marginal and eccentric dissidents in the colonies could find political validation in London—validation that could be translated into political power back in New England. On the strength of Gorton's efforts in London, Robert Rich, the Earl of Warwick and overseer of colonial affairs, extended the territory of Providence Plantations in New England to include Gorton's settlement at present-day Warwick, Rhode Island. Moreover, in the process of securing this patent in London, Gorton refined the practice of colonial dissent. Cannily representing, or misrepresenting, affairs far over the horizon, Gorton transformed his followers from squatters to martyrs, and himself from a Massachusetts convict into a Rhode Island founder.

To do so, Gorton produces a New England dissenting narrative that is an explicit, transatlantic appeal in print for political mediation. With the publication of *Simplicities Defence against Seven-Headed Policy*, (1646) Gorton fuses religious polemic and civil protest into a coherent expression with political force in a transatlantic milieu. What is striking about Gorton's campaign is that he prevails in a volatile time not by offering a new model of colonial privileges and obligations or other radical reform, but rather by an almost atavistic appeal to traditional lines of authority, devolving to a statement of his rights as an English subject, regardless of his physical location. He presents his persecutions as an intrusion by Massachusetts into the proper relation of state and subject.

Gorton has not been lucky in his chroniclers. To a surprising degree, the most recent accounts of his career recapitulate the limitations of the earliest. In London, Gorton quickly caught the eye of Presbyterian heresiographers eager to include a New England specimen in the taxonomies of heretics they produced to affirm the need for Presbyterian supervision of religion, and since then his story has rarely escaped this context of heresiography.

What attention Gorton has attracted in recent scholarly literature echoes the approach of seventeenth-century Scots heresiographers. In the wake of a generation of influential studies of colonial New England culture that emphasized consensus and orthodoxy, scholars who do engage the activities of heterodox colonists tended to view challenges to authority with the understanding that orthodoxy feeds on dissent, codifying and reinforcing itself. Even Philip Gura, whose *Glimpse of Sion's Glory* is the most extensive treatment of religious radicalism in seventeenth-century New England, sees few moments when radical opinion prevailed at all, and suggests that the presence of clearly heterodox persons spurred an orthodox majority to pull together all the more. He summarizes Gorton's career with this prim assertion: "In moving against Gorton they moved one step farther toward the summoning of the second synod, which would codify their understanding of Puritanism. He could not be tolerated, but he could be used."[3]

In this and other accounts, New Englanders of the 1640s seem to be living in Camelot compared with their king-killing, leveling, ranting, pamphleteering, tub-preaching brothers and sisters in England. The galaxy of political and religious radicals populating the London of Christopher Hill's *The World Turned Upside Down* or the texts populating Nigel Smith's *Perfection Proclaimed* seem to be almost absent from the American scene.[4] Gorton, however, was able to create a home for his radical ideas in New England Manipulating his audiences, and the notion of audience itself, Gorton forges surprising links between his own interests and those of the overseers of colonization, as he presents London with a public narrative of his career in New England that reinvents the structures of political power and clerical authority, there by questioning the legitimacy of the authority the Bay Colony claimed.

I: "A Sordid Man"

Samuel Gorton's early career in New England is not what one might expect of someone who would manage to solicit the favor of powerful political leaders in England. Indeed, from his arrival in New England, Gorton managed to infuriate nearly everyone he encountered. Gorton was born in the late 1590s, did not attend college, and worked as a clothier in London as an adult. He came with his wife to the Massachusetts Bay Colony in the winter of 1636–37, evidently laboring under the misapprehension that the young colony was a citadel of religious freedom. He arrived during the Antinomian Controversy, and quickly departed for Plymouth, seeking more congenial neighbors. His lay religious gatherings in Plymouth attracted a few adherents, but Gorton was soon expelled from the colony in the wake of a dispute with his landlord, Plymouth preacher Ralph Smith, over the behavior of Gorton's servant, accused of "smiling during the Sabbath meeting."[5]

In 1638, Gorton repaired to the settlement at Pocasset, now Portsmouth, Rhode Island, which had just been settled by a number of Antinomians exiled from Massachusetts, including Anne Hutchinson. His religious teachings drew him more followers, and he assumed a role in the government of the nascent colony. Again, a dispute involving a servant in his household landed him in the infant court at Portsmouth, where he called the justices "just asses," and otherwise abused William Coddington, the governor of the English settlements on Aquidneck, in a way that guaranteed his exile from the island—and earned him a whipping, by some accounts. In late 1641, Gorton sought refuge in Providence, where he and his growing band of followers managed to irritate even the famously tolerant Roger Williams, who complained to Winthrop of Gorton's "bewitching and bemadding" carriage. Gorton's party settled at Pawtuxet, on the outskirts of Providence, near the settlements of Robert Cole and William Arnold, who previously had been convicted by the Massachusetts courts as a drunkard and a Sabbath breaker, respectively.[6]

Despite being clearly outside the bounds of the Bay Colony patent, which ran from three miles north of the Merrimack River to three miles south of the Charles River, Cole and Arnold sought the protection of the Massachusetts government, which moved the Bay Colony authorities to claim jurisdiction in the area, and eject Gorton. After an exchange of obstreperous letters with the Bay Colony, Gorton moved further south, purchasing from Narragansett Indian sachems in 1643 a tract on Narragansett Bay on a neck of land known as Shawomet. The Bay Colony, claiming that the land belonged to different, lesser sachems, who also had submitted to Massachusetts jurisdiction, again called for Gorton's party to leave. More letters followed, culminating in a military expedition that captured Gorton and carried him to trial in Boston in the fall of 1643.

Gorton narrowly escaped execution for the blasphemous nature of his retorts to the Bay Colony and was sentenced to labor in irons, as were several of his confederates. Because Gorton's mouth was not shackled, this arrangement proved to be at least as onerous for captor as for captive, and in early 1644, Gorton's sentence was commuted to banishment, which included ejection from his settlement at Shawomet. After a brief sojourn back in Aquidneck, Gorton set out for London to appeal his case to the overseers of the English colonies. The published version of this appeal survives as *Simplicities Defence against Seven-Headed Policy.*

II: "A More Full View of Things"

The bulk of *Simplicities Defence* is essentially an annotated documentary history of the dispute between Gorton's party and the Massachusetts Bay Colony. In this context, it provides the same kind of evidentiary grist for scholarship on this affair as David D. Hall's *The Antinomian Controversy: A Documentary History* does for the Antinomian Controversy, or would have, had it been prepared at the time, and from documents prepared by Antinomians and copiously and tendentiously annotated.

The conflict had simple enough beginnings. The Massachusetts Bay Company informed Gorton's party that they considered the party to be encroaching on its patent. A move from the precincts of Providence to Warwick (then called Shawomet) did not satisfy Massachusetts, and letters continued to pass back and forth between Gorton's party and Massachusetts. As the exchange unfolds, Gorton's rejoinders are long and bewildering, while Massachusetts' are terse and emphatic. Ultimately, the Gorton party's intransigence moved the Bay Colony to send an armed party to Shawomet (via Providence, to the consternation of its residents). This force seized Gorton, and carried him back to Boston for trial.[7]

The offense that prompted the actions against Gorton was trespassing alleged by the Bay Colony, but the trial of Gorton and his followers was on charges of blasphemy. As Winthrop explains, in the course of their exchanges, "twelve of the English . . . have subscribed their names to horrible and detestable blasphemies."[8]

It was in a secular realm, however, that Gorton's dissent from the Bay colony had the most impact. The final section of *Simplicities Defence* is the most innovative, not only in its themes, but also in its very existence. This final portion describes Gorton's career after he passes through the Bay Colony judicial system. Unlike many both before and after him, Gorton escaped the Massachusetts courts with his body and dissenting voice intact. This portion of the story challenges the narrative structure the Bay Colony justice system attempts to impose on the dissident, where the final chapter is always and inevitably punishment: The story of the Antinomians circulated by the Bay Colony, with its "Rise, Reign, and Ruine" structure, is typical of this tendency. Gorton is arrested, tried, convicted, imprisoned, and then turned loose. It is a narrative that cannot be contained by the judicial apparatus of courtroom and cell, followed by the gallows or banishment. The very appearance of Gorton's story in London, in Gorton's words, would suggest to readers there that Massachusetts courts cannot contain Gorton.

To say the least, Gorton's experience was unusual in New England. Generally, when a New Englander fought the law, the law won, victories the magistracy shared with a London audience. As an example, in Winthrop's *A Short Story of the Rise, Reign, and Ruine of Antinomians, Familists and Libertines,* the wheels of justice grind inexorably to silence Anne Hutchinson and her adherents. Hutchinson is detained, tried, convicted, exiled, and killed by Indians, an event that Thomas Weld places squarely within the scope of a larger justice working in concert with the Massachusetts magistrates: "Thus did the Lord heare our groanes to heaven, and freed us from this great and sore affliction."[9] The Indian tomahawk is merely an extension of the judicial system, preserving the Bible Commonwealth and bringing Hutchinson's tale to a timely close. In a different vein, the triumphalist narratives of the Pequot war published in London echo the same articulation of New England power and righteousness on a London stage.

In microcosm, then, this final portion of *Simplicities Defence* mirrors the discursive work of Gorton's career as a whole. Like Ishmael, he alone escapes to tell the tale, and it is also in this final section that Gorton makes his most dramatic contribution to the evolution of transatlantic discourse—he turns the Indians not into Christian believers but English subjects. Anne Myles points to Gorton's "construction of [Indian] native subject" as allowing "the beset Narragansetts [to] see themselves as being in analogous condition to destitute whites" who "can now when they write to the Massachusetts General Court state pointedly that they expect the colony's 'former love' to increase, since by their deed they have become 'subjects now... unto the same King.'"[10] However, it is in the context of Gorton's appeal to England that this assertion appears, and it is in the context of a London, not a Boston, audience that Gorton claims this power for the Narragansetts, and himself.

The disposition of the native inhabitants of New England was of great interest both to New England writers and to their audiences in England; in almost every Stuart colonial charter, bringing the heathen to Christ is listed as one, if not the central, aim of colonization. As colonial affairs unfolded, Native Americans emerge as an important way to talk about the success of one's settlement. Despite an initial charge to share their Christian faith with the Indians, Bay Colony ministers and magistrates seem to have ignored their neighbors as much as possible until the success of

Roger Williams's *Key into the Language of America* spurred them to make some success of their own to report to London.

In these responses, the Bay Colony's engagement with Native Americans is represented as fundamentally evangelical: enumerating souls won is how it recorded its success. Conversions were breaking news, as it were, rushed to print in London at the first possible opportunity. Notably, *New Englands First Fruits* (1643/4) foreshadows the approach of the later Eliot Tracts in celebrating the progress of the Gospel in New England. In addition to challenging Williams's Indian account, Bay Colony apologists could also deploy evangelical successes as a leaven for more disturbing news coming out of the colony. Thus, at the end of his introduction to the third edition of *A Short Story*, Weld adds to his introduction: "I think it meet for to add a comfortable passage of newes from those parts written to me very lately by a faithfull hand . . . . That two Sagamores (or Indian Princes) with all their men women and children, have voluntarily submitted themselves to the will and law of our god . . . and have for that end put themselves under our government and protection."[11] The timing of this comment indicates that these "Sagamores" were, in fact, Pomham and Sacononoco, whose appeal offered a pretext for the expedition against the Shawomet setters. This irony underscores the narrowness of the Massachusetts Bay Colony's representative strategy for Native Americans: For Winslow, and other Bay Colony apologists, narrating a christening and conformity to Bay Colony laws seemed to be the beginning and end of the engagement with Native Americans that Boston ministers and magistrates could imagine.

With less coercive force at their command, the dissenting settlers of southern New England had to be considerably more creative, not only in their encounters with Native Americans, but also in their representations of them. As we saw in the previous chapter, Roger Williams produced *A Key into the Language of America*, a guide to Indian language, culture, and mores, which took the revolutionary step of recognizing Native American communities as legitimate, civil societies, rather than troops of nomadic, heathen savages.[12] To preserve his home in Shawomet, Gorton effects a similar transformation, in a political, rather than cultural, realm.

On his return to Narragansett Bay from Boston, Gorton and his followers still faced banishment from their homes and fields on Shawomet. After their release, these settlers inquired "The order of your Court last held, being dark and obscure . . . we may not therefore forebear to require an explanation of what you intend by [banishment from] the lands of Pomham and Sacononoco, for we know none they had, or ever had, under your jurisdiction."[13] This is a disingenuous reference to lands well known to the settlers: "if you should therefore so far forget yourself, as to intend thereby our land lawfully bought, and now in our possession, and inhabited by us, called Shawomet . . . we resolve upon your answer to wage law with you, and try to the uttermost, what right or interest you can show to lay claim, either to our lands or our lives."[14] Winthrop's reply was predictably unequivocal: "The expression and intent of the order of our last general court, concerning your coming within any part of our jurisdiction, doth comprehend all the lands of Pomham and Sacononoco, and in the same are included the lands which you pretended to have purchased . . . be the place called Shawomet or otherwise, so as you are not to come there, upon peril of your lives."[15]

Faced with the threat of death if he dares return home, Gorton performs a brilliant piece of improvisation, appropriating and surpassing the hegemonic technique of his Bay Colony rivals. In the face of a volatile situation among whites, Narragansetts, Mohegans, and smaller tribes, it behooved Pomham and Sacononoco to seek the protection of Massachusetts, just as it behooved the Bay Colony to extend its influence toward the Narragansett Bay, and the submission of Pomham and Sacononoco to the authority of the Massachusetts Bay government accomplished both ends. As Winthrop noted in his journal, "This we did partly to rescue the men from unjust violence, and partly to draw in the rest in those parts, either under ourselves or Plymouth." In a classic statement of early American Realpolitik, Winthrop observes that "the place was likely to be of use to us, especially if we should have occasion to send out against any Indians of Narragansett and likewise for an outlet into Narragansett Bay, and seeing that it came without our seeking, and would be no charge to us, we thought it not wisdom to let it slip."[16]

Gorton imaginatively improves on this strategy of extending power through the submission of neighbors from the context of a local squabble to the full expanse of colonial power. Describing his return among his Indian friends, Gorton indicates their surprise at his safe return from the jaws of so powerful a foe: "The Indians of that great country of the Narragansetts, hearing of our return without loss of our lives, they wondered, having observed the causeless cruelty they had offered unto us . . . they marvelled much at our deliverance and release."[17] This wonder enables Gorton to exploit another aspect of the Massachusetts campaign against him: "Now our countrymen having given out formerly, amongst the Indians, that we were *not Englishmen*, to encourage them against us . . . they then called us Gortoneans."[18] Gorton's insistent Englishness is at the core of his suit in London, but he is able to turn this rhetorical exile by Massachusetts to his advantage by translating it into an Indian language: "Now the Indians calling the English in their language, Wattaconogues, they now called us Gortonoges."[19] Ventriloquized into the mouths of Indians, this distinction empowers Gorton's party, making the actions of the Bay Colony against a dissident appear to be a struggle between Wattaconogues and Gortonoges. Here Gorton engages in "improvisation" in the sense Stephen Greenblatt uses the word to identify the behavior of the Spanish colonists Peter Martyr describes, with an additional layer—Gorton is not simply manipulating Indians with his representation of himself, but manipulating his fellow English readers with his representation of how the Narragansetts understood his representation of himself.[20]

With this distinction in play, Gorton takes some liberties in relating contemporary events in England to his situation: "being that they heard a rumour of a great war in Old England . . . they presently framed to themselves a cause of our deliverance, imagining that there were two kinds of people in Old England, the one called by the name of Englishmen, and the other Gortonoges, and therefore the Massachusetts thought it not safe to take away our lives."[21] Because "the Gortonoges were a mightier people than the . . . Wattaconogues" even though "there were but few of us in New-England . . . yet that great people . . . that were in Old England would come over and put them to death that would take away our lives without just cause."[22]

On the strength of a narrow escape from the hangman in Massachusetts, Gorton persuades his Indian neighbors that he has influence far beyond immediate appearances. On the face of it, this is a variation on a stock scene from narratives of encounters between Europeans and native peoples: Appearing to summon forces beyond the comprehension of the natives, Europeans convince the Indians of their supernatural powers, and win them over.[23] However, the real audience for this performance by Gorton is the sachems of Parliament, and not the lords of Narragansett Bay, and thus Gorton turns the admiration of the Indians into political capital he can carry with him to London.

Gorton explains to Parliament that his Narragansett neighbors were so impressed by the English power Gorton embodied that they sought to align their own polity with this authority. The result is one of the more curious documents in the literature of the Anglophone encounter with

Native Americans, and a tour-de-force by Gorton in its re-imagination of the contours of political authority. In its scrupulous appropriation of the language of treaties to an unforeseen end, it is worth reading at length, but what is excerpted here conveys the sense and tone of the whole. Gorton does not persuade the Indians to accept Christ as their savior, but rather Charles I as their sovereign.

> Know all Men, Colonies, Peoples and Nations . . . we the chief Sachems, Princes or Governors of the Narragansett . . . do upon serious consideration, mature and elaborate advice and counsel, great and weighty grounds and reasons moving us hereunto, whereof the one most effectual unto us, is, that noble fame we have hear of that GREAT AND MIGHTY PRINCE, CHARLES, KING OF GREAT BRITAIN, in that honorable and princely care he hath of all his . . . true and loyal subjects; the consideration whereof moveth and bendeth our hearts with one consent, freely, voluntarily, and most humbly to submit, subject, and give over ourselves, peoples, lands and rights . . . unto the protection, care and government of that WORTHY AND ROYAL PRINCE CHARLES KING OF GREAT BRITAIN AND IRELAND.[24]

By 1644, Charles I had more pressing concerns than the protection and care of a tribe of Indians an ocean away, but the submission spells out a very specific reason for this resort to England: The Indians desire to be "ruled and governed according to the ancient and honorable laws and customs, established in that so renowned realm and kingdom of Old England."[25] Gorton's concern for the traditions and precedents of English common law is manifest throughout *Simplicities Defence* and the rest of his work; the role he doubtless played in preparing this document, putatively the production of Indian sachems, is nowhere more evident.

This insistence on English law also had tangible benefits for these Native supplicants; as the document asserts, this direct submission to the King removed the Massachusetts Bay Colony from the judicial equation. The submission is "upon condition of his Majesty's royal protection, and righting of us in what wrong is, or may be done unto us . . . not that we find ourselves necessitated hereunto in respect of our relation . . . with any of the natives in these parts . . . but have just cause of jealousy and suspicion of some of His Majesty's pretended subjects."[26] In this event, the sachems, through Gorton, seek "to have our matters and causes heard and tried according to his just and equal laws, in that way and order His

Majesty shall please to appoint."[27] Finally, and critically, "Nor can we yield over ourselves unto any that are subjects themselves in such a case."[28] What is presented as a unilateral gesture of homage to the power of King and Parliament is, in fact, a canny effort to inaugurate the sort of direct, provincial system of colonial supervision that began to emerge only after the Restoration. Despite deep-seated resentment of this system in much of New England, Gorton and his fellows might well imagine less to fear from such a system than from the continued attentions of their neighbors in Massachusetts, Plymouth, and Connecticut.

With this creative legal gambit, Gorton assists the Narragansett sachems in claiming autonomy in the face of further legal aggression by Massachusetts. There is no question that Gorton and his fellows played the major role in drafting this submission; setting aside questions of Indian literacy, the document parrots formal English legal language too much to be produced by anyone unfamiliar with English courts. It is safe to assume that the document was prepared by Gorton or an associate and signed by the sachems with their various marks.

The question of informed consent is vexed for any document prepared by a European for an Indian to sign, especially at such an early stage of the contact between English and Native American cultures. That the signatures of Pessicus, Conanicus, Mixan, and their witnesses must be represented graphically, rather than in type, suggests the incommensurability of English and Narragansett legal cultures. It is interesting to speculate to what degree the signers of this document—Pessicus, heir to the late Miantonomo; Conanicus, adviser to Miantonomo; Mixan, heir to Canonicus—understood what they signed, or how they understood the power to which they submitted. Anglo–Indian legal documents have become subject to richly deserved scorn as examples of white duplicity and greed; in this period, Francis Jennings has detailed some of the ruses used to steal land from Native Americans under the rubric he calls "the deed game."[29] Despite more cordial dealings with the Native Americans than Massachusetts managed, Gorton does not escape Jennings's criticism. In this case, however, what Gorton seeks was more abstract than a title to a piece of land—he is describing the relation of one form of authority to another, echoing both his theological concerns and political struggles.

The knowledge of Roger Williams's triumphant return to Providence with a charter is echoed in Gorton's activities in the last section of *Simplicities Defence*; as Williams carried the knowledge set down in the *Key* back with him to London, so Gorton carries the document of this submission

our dreed Soveraigne, and that according to the English mens account. Dated the nineteenth day of *Aprill*, One thousand six hundred forty foure.

Pessicus his Marke, Chiefe Sachim and Successor of that late deceased *Myantonomy*.

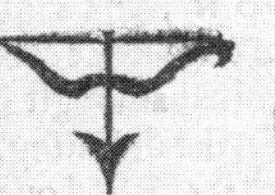

The Marke of that Ancient *Conaunicus*, Protector of that late deceased *Myantonomy*, during the time of his nonage.

The Marke of *Mixan*, son and heir of that above-said *Conaunicus*.

Witnessed by two of the chiefe Counsellors to Sachim *Pessicus*.

Indians {

AuWashoosse his Mark

Tomanick his Mark

Sealed and delivered in the presence of these persons

English: { *Christopher Helme.* *Robert Potter.* *Richard Carder.*

Here

FIGURE 6: From Samuel Gorton,
Simplicities Defence against Seven-Headed Policy (London: 1646).
Courtesy of Houghton Library, Harvard College Library US 10867.1.*

back with him to the same effect. In fact, the language of the submission calls for just such an act: "we have, by joint consent, made choice of four of his loyal and loving subjects, our trusty and well-beloved friends, Samuel Gorton, John Wickes, Randall Holden, and John Warner, whom we have deputed, and made our lawful Attornies or commissioners, not only for the acting and performing of this our deed, but, in behalf of his highness; but also for the safe custody, careful conveyance and declaration thereof unto his grace."[30] With this document, Gorton not only brings Indian subjects into the English realm; he also connects his remote corner of North America to the same authority empowered to rule in his case.

Of course, Charles I did not see this submission from the Narragansett sachems during the interval between its delivery to London and his execution. In this light, the submission might seem to strike rather the wrong note. However, because control of the colonies was one of many royal powers Parliament arrogated to itself in the early days of the revolution, the Committee for Foreign Plantations was pleased to receive this document, and to act upon it in the King's stead. As the dedication to *Simplicities Defence* reveals, Gorton was acutely aware of who his patrons were; indeed, presenting the submission to the Parliamentary committee would have been a flattering recognition of their power in this matter.[31]

The order that the Commissioners issued in the case emphatically endorsed Gorton's representation of affairs in New England. Despite making conciliatory statements that Massachusetts's "spirits and affairs are acted by principles of prudence, justice, and zeal to God," the Commissioners reverse the judgment of the Bay Colony with respect to Shawomet and its inhabitants: "We find withal that the tract of land, called the Narragansett Bay . . . is wholly without the bounds of the Massachusetts patent granted by his majesty."[32] Gorton's expressions of patriotism inform this decision: "We have considered that they be English, and that the forcing of them to find out new places of residence will be very chargeable, difficult and uncertain."[33] Reinvesting Gorton's party with the rights and privileges of English subjects, the Commissioners enjoin Massachusetts to "permit and suffer the petitioners and all the late inhabitants of Narragansett Bay, with all their families and all such as hereafter shall join with them, freely and quietly to live and plant upon Shawomet, and such other parts of the said tract of land within the bounds mentioned . . . without extending your jurisdiction to any part thereof."[34] This patent from the commissioners is the foundation of the Shawomet plantation's freedom from the legal and military aggression of its Puritan neighbors. In gratitude, the Shawomet setters renamed their home after the Earl of Warwick on their return.

Describing a contemporaneous episode in transatlantic print culture, Grantland Rice notes the ability of dissident authors like John Child "to circumvent the Puritan theocracy's rigorous attempt to contain a rapidly expanding print sphere . . . [by] exploiting . . . two extraordinary periods for press freedom in seventeenth-century England." Rice concludes that "writers like John Child . . . exposed their dissenting views to a wider reading public, leveraging political reform from abroad."[35] In Child's case, however, what Rice calls a "strategy of textual containment by offering a deconstructive sequel" made "interpretation of the 'Jonas' story the primary site of contestation in the pamphlet, suggest[ing] the difficult position dissenting writers faced in voicing their claims."[36] Because there was no sermon from Cotton or another minister forestalling *Simplicities Defence*, Gorton's texts were less susceptible to this kind of attack; instead, Winslow's response serves mainly to recirculate Gorton's grievances even as he labors to refute them in *Hypocrisie Unmasked*.

In essence, Gorton escapes the discursive monopoly the Bay Colony magistracy attempted to hold over New England by publishing in London, and considering their effort to quash Child's criticism of Massachusetts, it is not at all surprising that the Massachusetts court moved to send its own representative to counter Gorton's claims. The choice of Winslow for the job was fitting, for he was an established figure in colonial affairs. He published one of the earliest narratives of Puritan settlement in the New World, *Good Newes from New England*, from 1624, and had a hand in the 1622 *Mourt's Relation*. Additionally, as a pillar of the Plymouth settlement deputed to speak for Massachusetts, he embodied the collective scorn the United Colonies held for Gorton.

Winslow was as qualified as any to answer Gorton, but he lacked the rhetorical wherewithal to outflank him. The body of *Hypocrisie Unmasked* takes a documentary form similar to *Simplicities Defence*, but it also apes Winthrop's account of the Antinomian Controversy, *A Short Story of The Rise, Reign, and Ruine of Antinomians, Familists and Libertines* (1644), in its production of lengthy lists of errors gleaned from Gorton's letters. In effect, Winslow's rebuttal of *Simplicities Defence* is a tedious gainsaying of Gorton's text.

Winslow's effort to contain Gorton presumes a rhetorical authority over American affairs that had already begun to erode. Winthrop's *A Short Story* relies in part on a similar strategy of enumerating errors, but such a strategy presumes a monopoly on the truth, a privilege which fewer and fewer London observers were willing to grant to Massachusetts. The high-handed conduct of the Bay Colony in quashing the Antinomian Controversy attracted unfavorable attention from London observers, while Gorton's eccentric beliefs were unexceptional in a London teeming with sects and within the pale of the New Model Army's spectrum of beliefs.[37]

The doctrinal leeway available to Gorton is evident in an incident he discusses in a rejoinder he addressed to Nathaniel Morton in response to his *New Englands Memorial,* where Gorton is termed a "pestilent seducer," among other epithets. Discussing his preaching in London, Gorton asserts that "Indeed once in London three or four malignant persons caused me to be summoned before a committee of Parliament because I was not a university man; I appeared and my accusers also." Ultimately, and after Winslow's refusal to prefer religious matters against Gorton, his "answers and arguments were honourably taken by the Chairman and the rest of the Committee and my selfe dismissed as preacher of the Gospell . . . . Which act of that committee I take to be as good an humane call to preach as any of your ministers have."[38] Acquittal on charges of preaching without a license is a peculiar sort of ordination, and as Gorton's account is the only surviving record of this affair, the actual circumstances are difficult to determine. Unless Gorton made up this story out of whole cloth to buttress his rejoinder to Morton, which seems unlikely, the sum of the story is that Gorton's heterodoxy was below the threshold of what would move Parliament to act against him. The fundamentally different religious cultures of London and Boston in the mid-1640s diminished the threat Gorton posed in London, even as they magnified the threat he posed in New England.

III: "Suffer Mr. Gorton to Pass"

According to Gorton, Winslow declined to testify about Gorton's preaching because "his businesse with me lay before another Committee of Parliament."[39] The extent of Winslow's success in pressing his complaint was to secure a hearing for himself and Gorton before the Commissioners in 1647, to review their decision on Shawomet. As they announced to Winthrop, "we have spent some time in hearinge bothe partes, concerning the boundes of these Patentes," but "we could not, at this distance, give a Resolution."[40] With other affairs pressing on them, the Commissioners confirmed the status granted to Gorton's settlement the previous year, and counseled the colonies to co-exist harmoniously. Ultimately, the actions of the Committee for Foreign Plantations on Gorton's behalf worked more by restraining Massachusetts than by privileging Gorton—he is given the liberties due any English subject, to the Bay Colony's dismay. These instruments do not flatter Gorton as Roger Williams was flattered by references to his "Printed Indian Labours" in the Providence charter, but do satisfy Gorton's goals in making his appeal. Indeed, in this practice of checking Massachusetts, and in permitting Gorton to continue what he had been doing, they reflect the scenario Gorton constructs throughout— he is a loyal English subject who simply seeks to enjoy the privileges of any such, without the molestations of neighbors. Thus, the Committee for Foreign Plantations essentially defines Warwick, Rhode Island, negatively, as the territory that Massachusetts cannot claim for itself from an English subject. However, in limiting the compass of Bay Colony power and in extending English subjectivity across the Atlantic, the Committee for Foreign Plantations confirms Gorton's view of the relation of colonists, colonies, and colonial authority.

This support of Samuel Gorton by the architects of the English Puritan migration to America mandates a reconsideration of Gorton, these colonial leaders, and the nature of migration itself. Attention to these overseers of colonial policy has diminished in contemporary scholarship of New England. In a parallel context, however, Karen Ordahl Kupperman's study of the Providence Island Company points out the importance of London colonial government. Conveniently, many members of the Committee for Foreign Plantations (C.F.P.) were Providence Island Company veterans, and some estimate of their inclinations in New England can be gleaned from their conduct concerning Providence Island. Beyond Gorton's belletristic gesture of dedicating *Simplicities Defence* to Warwick, the Earl and his fellows comprise the immediate and most important audience for Gorton's performance. As this reading of *Simplicities Defence* depends critically on a sense of who responded to it, and where, a reconstruction of Gorton's Parliamentary supporters is in order. There are four critical documents Gorton elicited from this committee: one, the order restoring Warwick to Gorton's party of 15 May 1646; two, the order giving them free passage from any New England port to their homes, also drafted on 15 May 1646; three, the declaration of the C.F.P.'s intent to adjudicate the claims of Winslow and Gorton of 25 May 1647; and four, the

final determination by the C.F.P. that the issue of the rival claims cannot
be decided at such a distance, and thus to confirm the original order, allowing the Gortonists to remain, of 22 July 1647.[41]

Table 1 details the signers of the various instruments Gorton secured
from Parliament in his struggle with Massachusetts, and from the original
members of the Committee for Foreign Plantations. Unfortunately, we
face many of the same difficulties in reconstructing Gorton's supporters
that he faced himself in constructing this coalition. There are not surviving documents indicating which members of Parliament supported Winslow's countersuit, as we have for the rival Williams and Weld–Peter suits,
so we can identify Gorton's supporters with more confidence than we can
his opponents. In short, it is difficult to interpret the meaning of the absence of a signature. As a rule, the members of the C.F.P. were extensively
involved in a press of domestic, political, and (prior to the Self-Denying
Ordnance) military affairs. As Raymond Stearns describes in his reconstruction of the signers of Weld and Peter's unsuccessful Narragansett
Patent, colonial appeals were neglected for months while members of the
committee were absent from London on military campaigns.[42] Thus, the
absence of a name may indicate either explicit disapproval of Gorton's suit,
or it may indicate simply absence. While it is difficult to make conclusive
judgments about a given CFP member's endorsement of Gorton based
on the presence or absence of a signature, it is reasonable to conclude that
the presence of a name on one or more of these documents indicates support for Gorton's suit, at least when measured against the counterclaims
of Massachusetts.

With this caveat in mind, the character of Gorton's support is still
quite unexpected. The original members of the C.F.P. who sign one or
more of the letters favorable to Gorton are Robert Rich, Earl of Warwick
(1587–1658); Philip Herbert, Earl of Pembroke (1584–1650); Edward Mon-
tagu, Earl of Manchester (1602–1671); William Fiennes, Lord Saye and
Sele (1582–1662); Arthur Hasselrige (d. 1661); Benjamin Rudyer (1572–
1658); Dennis Bond (d. 1658); Miles Corbet (d. 1662); Cornelius Holland
(d. after 1660); and Samuel Vassal (1586–1667). These men are among
the most active participants in colonial schemes, and interlocked in any
number of overlapping ventures. Warwick had been involved in colonial
undertakings for most of his life, and supported clergy of very diverse convictions through the livings in his gift.[43] Warwick's interest in Gorton's
case might have been animated by this same heterodox generosity; at the
same time, the grant of Shawomet to Gorton also might have represented

a convenient way to trammel an increasingly intransigent Bay Colony, and to articulate the C.F.P.'s authority in colonial affairs.

Gorton's support is diverse enough that it is impossible to make a statement along the lines of "by mobilizing the support of radical London politicians, Gorton was able to defend his claim to Shawomet against that of Massachusetts." Gorton's support defies easy political or religious characterization, but as David Underdown demonstrates at length in *Pride's Purge*, it is difficult to delineate consistent affiliations and associations for members of the Long Parliament even where domestic events are concerned.[44] In Gorton's case, his most enthusiastic supporters are distributed among Underdown's categorizations of Revolutionary, Conformist, Abstainer, Secluded, and Imprisoned.[45] More fall into the first category than any other, but Gorton also enjoyed support from those who would soon be purged. It is tautological, but important, to recognize that the support Gorton found among from Parliamentarians came from men who were in positions of political power; Gorton's concern for hierarchy and the proper devolution of power goes a long way toward explaining the ability of this eccentric sectarian to attract political allies across a broad political spectrum. Against the chaos of London, and the pretensions of Boston, Gorton, for all of his eccentricities, presents himself as a colonist who knows his role, and will not exceed it—Gorton makes his claims on the basis of his status as a loyal English subject, not out of a sense of a special privilege.

Manchester and Pembroke were not intensely involved with colonial affairs, but were closely associated with Warwick and his family and were inclined to follow his lead on most matters concerning New England. Say and Sele, another veteran of many colonial schemes, was the only avowed Independent in the House of Lords, but was ill-disposed to Massachusetts after the rebuff of his colonial scheme, the "Proposal for Persons of Quality" in 1640.

Among the members of the House of Commons, Hasselrige was a close associate of Saye and of the late Lord Brooke, while Rudyer was associated with Pembroke, and followed in his wake. Denis Bond was later active in naval and trade issues under Cromwell, but a quiet member of this body. Cornelius Holland was also more active in the 1650s, and participated in the events leading to the execution of Charles I. Miles Corbet was perhaps the most radical of Gorton's supporters, an ardent Congregationalist and future regicide who would be executed after the Restoration. Vassal's relation to his brother William, who joined with John and Robert

TABLE 1: *Signers of documents relating to Samuel Gorton's dispute with the Massachusetts Bay Colony*

ORIGINAL CFP MEMBERS	GORTON PASSPORT, 15 MAY 1646	GORTON ORDER, 15 MAY 1646	LETTER TO MASS. CONCERNING GORTON, MAY 1647	TO, MASS., PLYMOUTH, AND CONN. RE WARWICK DISPUTE, JULY 1647	BIRTH AND DEATH DATES
Earl of Warwick		Warwick	Warwick	Warwick	1587–1658
Earl of Pembroke		Pembroke		Pembroke	1584–1650
Earl of Manchester		Manchester	Manchester	Manchester	1602–1671
Lord Saye & Sele			Saye & Sele		1582–1662
Lord Wharton					1613–1696
Lord Rolle/Roberts				Rolle	1598–1648
Gil. Gerard, Baronet					1587–1670
Sir Art. Hasselrige			Hasselrige	Hasselrige	d. 1661
Sir Henry Vane, Jr.					1613–1662
Sir Ben. Rudyer		Rudyer			1572–1658
John Pym					1584–1643
Oliver Cromwell					1599–1658
Dennis Bond		Dennis Bond			d. 1658

Source: SD 251	Source: JWJ 639–40	Source: JWJ 650–52	Source: JWJ 704	Source: JWJ 702	Source: DNB
Miles Corbet			Corbet	Corbet	d. 1662
Cornelius Holland	Holland	Holland	Holland	Holland	d. after 1660
Samuel Vassal	Vassal	Vassal			1586–1665?
William Spurstow					1605?–1666
	Nottingham	Nottingham			1621–1682
	Francis Dacre	Francis Dacre	Francis Dacre		1619–1662
	Alexander Rigby				1594–1650
	George Fenwick		Fenwick	Fenwick	1603–1657
	Francis Allein		Allein		d. 1658
	William Purfoye	Purfoye	Purfoye	Purfoye	1580?–1659
	Geo Snellinge	Snellinge		Snellinge	d. 1651
		Northumberland			1602–1688
		William Waller	Waller		1597–1668
				Henry Mildmay	d. 1664?
				Rich Salwey	1615–1685
			Basil Denbigh		1608?–1674

Note: SD = Simplicities Defence; JWJ = *The Journal of John Winthrop*; DNB = *Dictionary of National Biography*

Child as a remonstrant against the Bay Colony, explains his inclination to curtail Massachusetts power.

Absent, therefore, from Gorton's supporters in the original C.F.P. are Lord Wharton, Lord Roberts, Gilbert Gerard, Vane, Cromwell, and Spurstow. The absence of Vane's signature from all of these documents is surprising. While the birth, faith, and carriage of Gorton may have made him unpalatable to Vane, his persecution at the hands of the Massachusetts magistrates could not but have stirred sympathetic feelings from another victim of this oligarchy. He appears to have been present and active in Parliament in the late spring and early summer of 1646, when the C.F.P. acted to preserve Shawomet, and he exerted himself on Williams's behalf for the Providence charter, both in 1644 and in vacating Coddington's claim for Aquidneck in 1652. Williams was no admirer of Gorton, but likely would have preferred the annoyances that would attend his settlement to the threat that would attend having a Bay Colony outpost as a neighbor. There is no sign that Vane supported Winslow, so it is possible that the press of other affairs prevented Vane from exerting himself on Gorton's behalf: At the time, in May of 1646, he was busy with the Committee for Compounding, and the King went into the custody of the Scots on 5 May, or ten days before order on Gorton's behalf was issued.[46] In the absence of any direct evidence for the relation between Gorton and Vane, the reasons for the lack of Vane's support are difficult to ascertain.

Beyond the original members of the C.F.P., a number of additional members of Parliament took an interest in Gorton 1646–47, adding their signatures to one or more of the instruments supporting his case: Heneage Finch, Earl of Nottingham (1621–1682); Francis Dacre, Baron Dacre, or Francis Lennard (1619–1662); Alex Rigby (1594–1650); George Fenwick (1603–1657); Francis Allein (Allen) (d. 1658); William Purfoye (1580?–1659); George Snelling (d. 1651); Algernon Percy, Earl of Northumberland (1602–1688); William Waller (1597?–1668); Basil Fielding, Second Earl of Denbigh, (before 1608–1674); Henry Mildmay (d. 1664?); and Richard Salwey (1615–1685).

The striking feature of these supporters of Gorton is their moderation. Rather than constructing a radical coterie in London, Gorton manages to enlist holders of very different convictions to his cause. To be sure, some element of this success depends on qualities of personal charisma impossible to evaluate at this remove, especially in the absence of any contemporary accounts from his adherents. Surely, though, the same qualities that persuaded the settlers of Warwick to follow him in his peregrinations and persecutions served him in London. This ability to enlist support from unlikely sources is echoed in the publication of *Simplicities Defence*. The circulation of his story served him, but it may also have served other interests. The initial publication of *Simplicities Defence* was by Luke Fawne, who supported the Presbyterian cause, so his interest in the text may well have been in the discredit the book reflected on the Independent regime in Massachusetts, rather than in his sympathies for Gorton. Conversely, the second edition of *Simplicities Defence*, identical in substance save the title page, was published by George Whittington, a bookseller with more radical connections, including to Hannah Allen, who later married the notorious Livewell Chapman.[47] Gorton's story appealed to both Presbyterians and sectarians for the portrait it painted of an Independent party in control in Massachusetts but under fire in London.

During his sojourn in London, Gorton was active in the London Puritan underground, preaching at Thomas Lambe's church, to the consternation of Presbyterian heresiographers.[48] However, it does not appear that circulating in this religious milieu had much effect on his Parliamentary suit. The tub preachers and conventiclers were not the audience Gorton had to reach to preserve Shawomet, and his religious sphere appears to be almost entirely distinct from his political one. It is possible to draw some connections from Gorton, to New Model chaplains, to influential members of Parliament, but it is impossible, unfortunately, to make a specific argument, for instance, that it was Gorton's acquaintance with Paul Hobson, who enjoyed the patronage of Sir Arthur Hasselrige, that was the factor that carried the day.

At the same time, given his constant troubles in New England, it is hard to imagine that Gorton prevailed in London simply on the strength of his personal charm, though his dedication to Warwick demonstrates he was capable of a courtly gesture when so inclined. Instead, Gorton is able to attract support from London political leaders both to the left and right of the Bay Colony: For Presbyterians, Gorton's settlement could remain a thorn in the side of an Independent oligarchy; for more liberal-minded members of Parliament (M.P.s), Gorton's religious eccentricities did not outweigh his maintenance of an English identity and concern for proper political subordination. Gorton offered a more appealing model of colonial settlement than that of the dangerously independent-minded and intransigent Bay Colony, despite his religious views.

With this support, Gorton helps to unleash the diversity of religious and political opinion of mid-seventeenth-century England in the colonies (he was the first to write sympathetically of the New England Quakers) and finds concrete expression for this heterogeneity on the other side of the Atlantic. Gorton's Warwick and Winthrop's Boston emerge as two of a diverse assortment of settlements with different reasons, goals, and polities. From Providence Island in the Caribbean to the coast of Maine and beyond, a shifting coterie of lords, gentlemen, and merchants conceived and undertook a great number of different colonial projects, articulating divergent religious methods and aims. Samuel Gorton, for all of his personal and religious eccentricity, finds a way to present himself and his neighbors as English subjects, subject to colonial authority.

IV: Wresting Scripture

These texts, and the town of Warwick, are Gorton's legacy. Gorton was no Wesley, with a religious following persisting well after his death. As David Hall points out, Gorton, "the most prominent of the New England radicals . . . was unable to recruit more than a handful of 'Gortonists' and his group, which finally settled in Warwick, was dying out by 1670."[49] Notwithstanding Ezra Stiles's account of meeting the last surviving Gortonist in 1771, Hall's assertion that Gorton was not the face of popular religion in New England is well founded.[50]

However, it is expressly not the role of the dissident to represent the majority. Instead, Gorton's achievement is to find ways to use language to allow dissidents outside the majority to speak for themselves. Early on in his engagement with Gorton, John Winthrop commented of his party that "they were all illiterate men, the ablest of them could not write true English, no not common words, yet they would take upon them the interpretation of the most difficult places of scripture, and wrest them any way to serve their own turns."[51] However, Winthrop's complaint of Gorton's party's habit of "wresting scripture to serve their own turns" belies that it is facility with language that allowed Gorton and his adherents to thwart the aggression of Bay Colony ministers and magistrates. Nigel Smith and Elizabeth Skerpan point to genre as central to the literature of political revolution and radical religion in mid-seventeenth-century England, and it is in the context of genre that Gorton's more enduring contributions come to light.[52] Ranging between politics and religion, England and America, Gorton's texts shuttle from one of these concerns to the other, freeing Gorton to recast American religious debates in terms of English politics, or to interpret English religious debates in terms of American politics. In the following years, his approach was widely adopted by Quaker apologists seeking to check the persecution of their sect by the Bay Colony, as well as by those with secular grievances. In mixing the genres of colonial American discourse with those of English political and religious debates, Gorton demonstrates how differently minded American colonists could speak in a language that English power could authorize and imbue with political authority.

4. ANTINOMIANS, ANABAPTISTS, AND AQUIDNECK

Contesting Heresy in Interregnum London

I: The Coddington Coup

Samuel Gorton's errand secured the integrity of the mainland portion of the colony of Rhode Island and Providence Plantations, and, in the form of Gorton's passport, generated a rebuke to the Bay Colony for its high-handed relations with its neighbors. However, the island portion of the colony of Rhode Island, named Aquidneck by the Narragansetts, was a different matter. Antinomian exiles from the Bay Colony, voluntary and otherwise, settled the towns of Portsmouth and Newport on Aquidneck, and these towns faced a separate threat to its status as part of the colony of Rhode Island. William Coddington, who had been active in the Bay Colony government before departing in the wake of the Antinomian Controversy, sought to hijack the island's government and steer it in a more conservative direction. To this end, Coddington secured a commission from the Council of State, placing the island under his proprietary control.

It fell to John Clarke, a Baptist of Newport, to recover the island's government for the colony of Rhode Island and Providence Plantations. Thus, the context for Clarke's errand differs from Williams's and Gorton's—rather than solicit a new instrument of government, as Williams did, or confirm an earlier one, as Gorton did, Clarke had to persuade metropolitan authorities to undo an earlier instrument they had issued to a rival.

The aim of Clarke's errand was different from those of his precursors, but so were the means he used. In the transition from Williams and

Gorton's appeals to those of Clarke and then the Quakers, there are simultaneous shifts in content and form of the texts dissidents produced. Williams and Gorton manipulate representations of Native Americans to give their appeals leverage; Clarke and the Quaker apologists build on this technique to represent the English subject in America.

Where Williams and Gorton discover the value of metropolitan print as a site where it is possible to challenge colonial persecution, Clarke and the Quakers bring a new narrative self-consciousness to printed colonial dissent. Williams's ideological work is dispersed over a heterogeneous array of texts; Gorton's suit is in the form of an annotated anthology of the documents related to his case. For Clarke and the Quakers, there is a growing awareness that the experience of colonial persecution could be translated, through print, into metropolitan political capital. Thus, in place of Williams and Gorton's re-imagining of the relations between English and Native inhabitants of America, Clarke and the Quakers re-imagine power relations among English subjects.

These relations were in a state of flux when Clarke arrived in New England. Shortly after his arrival in Boston, Clarke joined a number of Bostonians who left the Bay Colony in the wake of the Antinomian Controversy and settled on Aquidneck, or the Island of Rhode Island. This common bond was not enough to prevent internal conflict, and a group left the original settlement at Portsmouth to settle Newport, on the south of the island. William Coddington was at the center of conflicts on Aquidneck. Despite his Antinomian sympathies, he was politically and socially conservative. He also appears to have been a snob, to judge by the discomfort his letters to Bay Colony leaders evinced about living among a group of outcasts. Unlike Williams, who maintained a correspondence with the Winthrops based on the assumption that they were equals, Coddington's correspondence with Bay Colony leaders has a servile and obsequious tone. Coddington made overtures to Bay Colony ministers and magistrates almost as soon as he settled in Newport. In early 1641, Coddington writes to John Cotton concerning his status in the Church of Boston, closing with "endeared affection to you and yours and all that remember us, I rest your neclected reiected afflicted frind Wm Coddington."[1] In a similar vein, Coddington wrote in 1646 to John Winthrop of John Winthrop, Jr.'s visit on his way south, telling him, "My purpose is er long to come to the Bay. I desire to be remembered to all that remember me."[2]

Coddington wrote from Newport. The charter Williams secured in

1644 embraced both his and Gorton's mainland settlements (Providence and Warwick, or Providence Plantations) and island (Rhode Island, or Aquidneck) portions of the colony, which contained the towns of Portsmouth and Newport. Coddington, however, did not cherish the relatively democratic constitution of the colony's mainland government, and sought to bring the island under a different rule of law. He made overtures to the United Colonies (an intercolonial confederation of Massachusetts, Plymouth, Connecticut, and New Haven), which rejected his overture because the group claimed the island was within the Plymouth patent.[3] These efforts failing, Coddington went to England, and managed to secure a commission granting him proprietary control of the island from the Council of State.

This commission had significance beyond the control of an island in Narragansett Bay. With the Island of Rhode Island under the proprietary control of Coddington, who was eager to compound with the United Colonies, there was a legitimate question of whether the colony charted in 1644 still existed and still offered any protection to Providence and Warwick from the ambitions of their neighbors. The Bay Colony had made incursions into Narragansett Bay on similarly flimsy pretexts in the past, as in the case of Samuel Gorton.

On a broader scale, an Aquidneck Island under Coddington's control had the potential to revise the narrative of New England history. If a moderate Antinomian rump on Aquidneck could be reintegrated into the United Colonies—effectively a satellite of the Bay Colony—the final chapter of the Antinomian Controversy would be cohesion, rather than fissure. There was a precedent for such a pattern—a portion of the Antinomian party followed John Wheelwright to settle Exeter, New Hampshire. Within a few years, this settlement, as well as the New Hampshire settlements of Portsmouth, Dover, and Hampton, were within the compass of the Bay Colony's power.[4] Thus, the northern portion of the Antinomian diaspora ultimately facilitated the Bay Colony's territorial expansion in that direction. Given previous efforts to secure land in and around Narragansett Bay, it is reasonable to assume that the Bay Colony would be only too happy to repeat this process of annexation to the south. Moreover, beyond the territorial and political advantages, absorbing Aquidneck would have the significant ideological advantage of re-integrating Antinomian exiles into the political structure of orthodox New England, thus producing a narrative that ends with a cohesive and solid orthodoxy, rather than irreparable fissures among English settlers in New England.

II: A Trip to Lynn

Because the grant of Aquidneck to Coddington threatened Rhode Islanders both on the mainland and on the island, both segments of the colony had a reason to seek a reversal of the grant to Coddington. Thus, two representatives traveled from Rhode Island to London to plead for the union of Rhode Island. Roger Williams represented the mainland Rhode Islanders concerned about the integrity of the colony, while Clarke represented Aquidneck residents opposed to Coddington's regime.

Before setting off for London, Clarke managed to get himself arrested in Lynn, Massachusetts. Along with fellow Baptists Obadiah Holmes and John Crandall, Clarke traveled to Lynn to visit William Witter, a Baptist there, and to conduct a religious service. They made no discernable effort to conceal their efforts, and two constables arrested Clarke and his party, carrying them to Lynn's church, where they refused to take part in the service. They were carried to trial at Boston, where they were convicted of "denying the lawfulness of baptizing infants," and "seducing the people of this Commonwealth from the truth of the Gospel of Jesus Christ," among other charges, and sentenced. Clarke faced a fine of twenty pounds, Crandall, five, and Holmes, thirty. If the men failed to arrange for these fines to be paid by the first day of the next Court of Assistants, they would be whipped instead.[5]

Religious persecution by the Bay Colony was not rare in this era; deliberately provoking it was, at least until the Quakers arrived in the late 1650s. The timing of events suggests that Clarke deliberately sought out this persecution. We do not know when Coddington returned, but it must have been between 3 April 1651, when he secured the commission in London, and early August, when Roger Williams shares the news of Coddington's return and commission with John Winthrop, Jr.[6] Clarke's excursion to Lynn occurred in mid-July, so it is probable, but not definite, that he set out for Lynn knowing of Coddington's coup. Presumably, being at Newport, he would have heard of the commission before Williams did, and Williams did not seem concerned to write Winthrop as soon as he heard the news, inasmuch as it comes near the end of a letter detailing many items.

Clarke embraced the Baptist tenets of believers' baptism and immersion no later than 1644, the Bay Colony's law against Anabaptists had been in place since 1644, and Witter had been at Lynn for several years before Clarke's visit. In the intervening years, however, Clarke had not previously been moved to make such a foray. The only other trip Clarke took on this kind of business was of a dramatically different nature: In the fall of 1649, he had traveled not to Lynn, a solid Puritan town deep in the Bay Colony, but to Rehoboth, an heterodox outpost of Plymouth on the border of Rhode Island, a town where religious discipline was hard to enforce, and from which he and fellow Baptist Mark Lucar returned without incident.[7] At Rehoboth, Clarke and Lucar, a former member of John Spilsbury's Baptist congregation in England, baptized Obadiah Holmes, who had clashed with Samuel Newman, the minister there. Clarke and Lucar returned from Rehoboth without incident, either because they were more discreet, or because of the absence of enforcement of the laws against Baptists. If the purpose of Clarke's trip to Lynn was simply to commune with a co-religionist, Clarke and his associates might have visited the elderly Baptist Witter in Lynn at any time in the several years previous, as Witter had been convinced of the insufficiency of the Bay Colony's ordinances of baptism for at least five years.[8] But on the eve of the most important action of his life, one that would determine the fate of the colony he founded, he was moved to travel into the heart of the Bay Colony and openly celebrate a forbidden religious ceremony.

To summarize, Clarke faced a distinct political challenge in Coddington's commission. Just before he went to make his case in London, he traveled to the Bay Colony and openly defied its religious laws, resulting in his arrest and trial, and the whipping of his companion. Unlike the Quakers who would arrive in New England at the end of the decade, Clarke did not make a habit of seeking out persecution—except on the eve of his departure for London. The evidence is circumstantial, but compelling—as a prelude to his errand, Clarke sought to manufacture an experience of colonial religious persecution that he could translate into metropolitan political capital.

III: A Trip to London

In London, Clarke circulates this capital in the form of *Ill Newes from New-England* (1652). *Ill Newes* is much more coherent and readable than *Simplicities Defence*, but retains some of its heterogeneous nature. The prefatory material consists of contains dedications to Parliament and the Council of State; the "Honored Magistracy, the Presbytery, and their dependency in the Mathatusets Colony in New-England"; the "true Christian Reader." Following the dedication is "a brief discourse touching New England, as to the matter at hand, and to that part of it, sci Rode Island, where my residence is, together with the occasion my going out with others from the Mathatusets Bay."[9] The body of *Ill Newes* consists of two parts: a narrative of the arrest, trial, and punishment of Clarke and his two friends, followed by a four-part Baptist apologetic, concluding with an assertion that "no servant of Jesus hath any authority from him to force upon others either their faith or the order of the Gospel of Christ. Wherein are produced eight arguments against persecution for case of conscience."[10]

The first section of this text narrates Clarke and Holmes's arrest and trial. Clarke offers a detailed account of his trial, similar to those in *Rise, Reign, and Ruine*, with the critical difference that it is the defendant, rather than representatives of the prosecution, who offers the narrative. As Gorton did, Clarke produces a printed version of the case he makes to London colonial authorities.

The heart of this narrative is a letter that Clarke publishes from Obadiah Holmes to London Baptist leaders William Kiffin and John Spilsbury. Holmes is the putative author of his own narrative of suffering, but it appears in the form it does through Clarke's offices, and Clarke appends his own narrative and several documents describing the aftermath of this punishment. In a limited way, Holmes and Clarke anticipate the authorial model of "suffering and subscribing" the Quakers developed.[11] We do not know what emendations Clarke may have made to Holmes's actual letter, or even definitively that Holmes wrote the letter that bears his name, but we do know that Clarke is ultimately responsible for the letter in the form in which it does appear. In his own letter, Holmes says, "what they laid to my charge, you may here read in my sentence."[12] The sentence does indeed appear in *Ill Newes*, but not in the letter, suggesting that Holmes was conscious that his letter would be part of a larger publication that Clarke would prepare in London. Evidently, Holmes furnished this letter to Clarke for his own use in *Ill Newes* as much as he intended it as a communication to Kiffin and Spilsbury.

Clarke makes the claim on his title page that "While old England is becoming new, New-England is become old," and this idea is the animating thesis of *Ill Newes*. English readers could see old England becoming new all around them, and the case of Obadiah Holmes furnishes Clarke with an opportunity to show just how New England was becoming old. As the charge is developed in the Holmes letter, the idea that New England is becoming old takes a much more specific form than a general implication that its first generation of leaders was old and out of touch with events in England. By "old," Clarke alludes to a period of just more than a decade ago: the heyday of Archbishop Laud's persecutions of nonconforming clergy and others. These terrors were well within the memory of any adult Londoner, and themselves echoed the more extreme persecutions of Protestants under Queen Mary in the previous century, which formed the bulk of the material for John Foxe's *Acts and Monuments,* colloquially known as "Foxe's Book of Martyrs."[13]

In recalling the Laudian persecutions of recent memory, Clarke has access to a vivid and recognizable body of literature that narrated these persecutions from the perspective of the sufferer, with disastrous effects for the persecutor. Henry Burton's *Divine Tragedie* (1636) and especially William Prynne's *A New Discovery of the Prelates Tyranny* (1641) offer Clarke a paradigm for accounts of punishments from the victim's perspective that subvert the state's intention and become powerful statements on behalf of the victim.[14] In her study of the rhetoric of this period, Elizabeth Skerpan shows that "the Laudian persecutions of 1637 reveal nothing less than a reversal of power through rhetoric."[15] Taken as a genre, narratives of Laudian persecutions, like many genres, offer a predictable narrative and a predictable result. Just as the ultimate outcome of a tragedy, romance, or mystery is rarely in doubt, no one picks up a narrative like Prynne's, Burton's, or Holmes's expecting that the victim of torture will recount learning the error of his ways through the ministrations of his inquisitors.

The most prominent of Laud's victims were Henry Burton, a minister; John Bastwick, a physician; and William Prynne, a lawyer. The trajectory of their persecution and triumph in the 1630s and 1640s, as described in their own narratives, furnished Clarke with an immediate model for the narrative of suffering at the hands of a persecuting government. For Laud's victims, the living presence of Foxe's book in English culture during the time of the Laudian persecutions meant that observers could easily revise punishments staged by the state into familiar scripts from the Book of Martyrs. As David Cressy points out, Henry Burton's account of William Prynne's first ear cropping in the *Divine Tragedie* (1636) "may have been influenced as much by his reading of Foxe's Book of Martyrs as by his witnessing of the scene at Westminster."[16] Cressy makes this comment as a way of questioning accounts of Prynne's "heroic forbearance" in the face of this barbaric punishment; more important, however, the striking uniformity of accounts of this affair demonstrates the power of

Foxe's heroes in shaping the perception, if not the reality, of the behavior of Laud's victims under duress of torture. John Knott observes of *A Briefe Relation*, the most extensive account of the persecution of Bastwick, Burton, and Prynne, that "what is most striking about the social drama the tract recreates is the self-conscious and skillful way that Bastwick, Burton, and Prynne appropriate language and gestures of martyrdom learned chiefly from Foxe."[17] Laud himself was so aware of the subversive potential of the Book of Martyrs that he refused to license a new edition in 1637.[18]

What made this form of dissent appealing to the successors of Bastwick, Burton, and Prynne was that it worked. The victims of Laud described their travails in a barrage of publications, most notably Prynne's *A New Discovery of the Prelates Tyranny* and *A Briefe Relation of Certaine Speciall and Most Materiall Passages and Speeches in the Starre Chamber* (1638/1641). The accounts of their sufferings won them the sympathies of many Londoners, even as these narratives worked to discredit Laud. Just after their public torment, the procession of the three to their respective prisons took on the air of a joyful parade—an occasion eclipsed only by their triumphant return to London, concurrent with the impeachment of Laud by the Long Parliament.[19]

For those who emulated them, one important legacy of this revision of Foxe's paradigm of martyrdom by Bastwick, Burton, and Prynne was their capacity to evoke the generic conventions of martyrologies without the inconvenience of dying. In England, John Lilburne uses this affair as a guide for narratives of his own suffering, and Clarke and Holmes are aware of its conventions as well.[20] Clarke left England in the late summer or early fall of 1637, and he was likely in London for the first phases of this saga; Holmes may still have been in England at this point. In any event, word of this affair quickly reached New England by other means: Henry Jessey, who would become a leading English Baptist, wrote to Winthrop in September 1637 with a detailed account of the sufferings of Bastwick, Burton, and Prynne. Jessey observes, "By these devices the Prelates hoped to have prevailed; but it is feared they have lost greatly by it. The poor credit they had with the vulgar is now quite lost."[21] Upon his return to England, Clarke very likely would have encountered this Baptist leader, and it is possible that Jessey reminded Clarke of the impact of this spectacle as he composed *Ill Newes*.

For Clarke's suit in London, the extra measure of persecution endured by Holmes is critical. Clarke's own experience of Massachusetts justice, while by no means pleasant, lacks the drama he needed to distinguish his dissenting narrative from individual personal gripes against the United Colonies, such as Morton's *New English Canaan* or Lechford's *Plain Dealing*; as Elizabeth Skerpan observes in the English context, one advantage of this genre of suffering evolving from Foxe was that "this discourse allowed the writer to represent himself as a spokesman for many, since it made his experiences not unique but exemplary."[22]

In the letter to Kiffin and Spilsbury, Holmes offers a narrative of suffering that works precisely because of its adherence to the generic conventions of martyrdom that were Anglicized by Foxe and revised by Laud's victims. Holmes begins his letter with a salutation to his brethren inquiring after the state of their souls and offers a brief account of his own spiritual journey, culminating in the trip to Lynn. The relation of Holmes's letter to the whole of *Ill Newes* echoes the placement of "Mr. Burton's heavenly and conformable speech" in *Briefe Relation*. Like Prynne, Clarke is as much disputant as victim, as in his lengthy agitation for a debate.[23] Burton furnishes Prynne with a sympathetic portrait of heroic suffering, which is what Holmes also offers Clarke. Clarke did not attempt to establish a typology explicitly linking each member of his party to one of the martyrs, but simply to suggest that the displacement of the suffering onto someone other than the narrator affords fresh opportunity to the narrator of persecution.

Burton's "Heavenly and Comfortable Speech" appears nearly unaltered from the 1638 to the 1641 version of *Briefe Relation*, and it stands out from the masses of documents and arguments Prynne compiles in this work as a memorable example of eloquent forbearance in the face of suffering. In *New Discovery*, at the sight of the pillory where he will lose his ears, Burton announces, "I see Mount Cavalry" and "Surely, if I be a Rogue, I am Christs Rogue, and no mans."[24] Upon the passage of his sentence, Holmes's response echoes the martyrological tradition explicitly: He tells the court, "I blesse God I am counted worthy to suffer for the name of Jesus."[25]

Many of the details common to the accounts of both Holmes's and Burton's punishment strain the credulity of all but the most sympathetic reader. However, the derivative quality of the narrative Holmes offers only underscores the self-conscious nature of this performance. At the pillory, Burton's friends offer him first aqua vitae (grain spirits), and then wine. He "needed it not; for I have, said he, (laying his hand upon his brest) the true water of life, which like a well doth spring up to Eternall life."[26] He frames his refusal of the proffered wine in similar terms. As he awaits the execution of his sentence, Holmes recounts that "many Friends came to visit me, desiring me to take the refreshment of Wine . . . but my resolution was not to drink Wine, nor strong drink that day until my punishment were over." The reason Holmes gives reveals as much about his self-conscious management of this spectacle as it does about his courage: "in case I had more strength, courage, and boldness, than ordinarily could be expected, the World should either say he is drunk with new Wine, or else that the comfort of the Creature has carried him through."[27] Holmes follows Burton's example of refusing drink, but Holmes refuses in order to shape the perceptions of his punishment, so that his heroic suffering will be a testimony to the strength of Jesus, not to the strength of the wine.

Holmes recounts the spiritual drama of the eve of the execution in more detail than Burton offers, but both accounts convey a sense of a near-supernatural visitation affording the endurance to confront the morning's events with courage.[28] Once on the stage of execution, Holmes offers an account that may indeed exceed Burton's in drama.[29] In place of the *Imitatio Christi* Burton deliberately develops in his interaction with his wife and retainers, Holmes has more contentious parleys with his executioners about the meaning of the day's event. Several times, Holmes asks to address the onlookers about his faith; when he is denied, he still manages to tell them, "that which I am to suffer for, is for the Word of God, and testimony of Jesus Christ." Increase Nowell, the magistrate charged with coordinating the execution of the sentence, retorts that the sentence is in fact for his "error, and going about to seduce the people."[30]

The awareness of an audience and the struggle for interpretation of these scenes manifest exceeds even the examples of Bastwick, Burton, and Prynne. In this respect, it is worth remembering that the entire punishment Holmes describes is one that he chooses for himself by refusing to have his fine paid. The structure of the torture Holmes suffers differs from those that his models suffer, and thus his narrative is framed differently as well. Rather than a time in the pillory and an ear cropping, Holmes is to suffer thirty strokes of a three-corded whip. The pillory makes a better pulpit than the whipping post does: Despite the intended discomfort, a prisoner can speak, and he likely has an audience for the length of his sentence.[31] Having one's ears cut off must be excruciating, but the pain is inflicted at once rather than over a period of several minutes. Holmes faces the distinct challenge of enduring great pain in front of an audience before his sentence is discharged. Nevertheless, according to the narrative Holmes forwards to England, he manages to beseech the Lord to forgive his persecutors, even as the blows fall upon him.[32]

Holmes prepares his spectators for the worst before his punishment, reminding them, "though my flesh should fail, and my spirit should fail, yet God would not fail."[33] Ultimately, God imbues flesh and spirit alike with the courage to resist: Released from the whipping post, Holmes chastises the magistrates for the severity of the punishment, even as he insists the strength of the Lord has made it ineffectual: "I told the magistrates, you have struck me as with Roses . . . though the Lord has made it easie to me, I pray God it may not be laid to your charge."[34] One imagines that Holmes was referring to the sweet blossoms of roses and not their thorny stems when he addressed the magistrates, and the imagery resonates with Burton's speech from the pillory: He had a nosegay with him, and a bee lit on its flowers, causing Burton to exclaim "Doe yee not see this poore Bee? She hath found out this very place to suck sweetness from flowers; And cannot I suck sweetnesse in this very place from Christ?"[35] Neither image, perhaps, is entirely credible, but both depend on the inversion of the bitterness of pain into the sweetness of Christ's love. In this context, it is no surprise that on the actual event of the ear cutting, "this Champion of Christ never once mooved or stirred for it."[36]

Describing the conventions of these narratives of suffering, Knott observes, "they embrace their suffering, exhort the onlookers, and demonstrate the strength of their faith by calmly enduring the punishment inflicted."[37] Holmes's letter includes all of these features, and also abides by a convention that Knott does not mention, that witnesses of the punishment will suddenly embrace the ideas that are being suppressed: Clarke appends documents describing the punishment of two men, John Spur and John Hazel, who comforted Holmes after his ordeal.[38] This sense of the contagion of dissent being spread by efforts to root it out is central to all of these narratives of punishment, for it is precisely the spectacle of public punishment in these narratives that turns public sentiment in favor of the criminal. In Burton's case, "the blood ran streaming down the scaffold, which divers persons standing about the Pillory seeing, dipped their handkerchers in, as a thing most precious."[39]

Beyond these immediate witnesses, the *Briefe Relation* also describes the warm reception the exiles received along the way to prison, especially William Prynne, whose picture was sold to his supporters at Chester, enraging the bishop.[40] Ultimately, of course, the sentiment in support of the three was so strong that one of the first acts of the Long Parliament was to free these three men and impeach Laud. In less dramatic if more direct terms, Clarke demonstrates that when Massachusetts whips a Baptist, two new Baptists appear. If the Bay Colony continues to punish dissent, it will be overrun with dissidents.

In their narratives, Bastwick, Burton, and Prynne turn "punishment into symbolic triumph in a scene that could have been scripted by Foxe."[41] For Clarke, the ultimate outcome lies outside the compass of his printed narrative, because the fate of his colony still hangs in the balance; more specifically, the fate of Aquidneck lies in the hands of the Council of State, to whom it falls to write the appropriate ending to Clarke's story.

IV: Undoing the Coup

Of course, all of the ability Clarke shows in using influential models to shape his discourse in England would be useless if he had no way to disseminate his message to sympathetic auditors with the power to intervene on behalf of Aquidneck. It is not possible to retrace the precise route of Clarke's access to the people with the power to provide the remedy he sought, but it is possible to situate Clarke in a web of powerful and influential Londoners that would enable him to reach the attentive and sympathetic audience he required for his suit to be successful.

One signal distinction between Clarke's suit and the earlier campaigns of Williams and Gorton was Clarke's Baptist faith. In place of Gorton's ill-defined mysticism and strong personal charisma and Williams's retreat into an eremitic spiritual life as a Seeker, Clarke espoused a recognizable, if not universally cherished, faith, known as Anabaptism to its opponents. Clarke devotes the final third of *Ill Newes* to a confession of the Baptist faith on behalf of himself, Holmes, and Crandall. testifying that first, "Jesus . . . is made both Lord and Christ;" second, "Baptism or dipping in water is one of the commands of this Lord Jesus Christ;" third, "every such servant of Jesus Christ . . . ought in point of duty to improve that talent which his Lord hath given him;" and fourth, "no servant of Christ Jesus hath any liberty, much less authority . . . to smite his fellow servant."[42]

This confession that Clarke offers London readers conforms in its general contours with the Confessions of 1644 and 1646 and with recorded practice of Baptist congregations in London at the time of his visit. The details of his practice in New England before this visit cannot be reconstructed very accurately, but it seems likely that the confession he published might have been influenced by his encounters with Baptists in England. The more immediate question is of what role Clarke's Baptist faith played in his campaign on behalf of Aquidneck. Certainly, the England of Cromwell was a more hospitable place for Baptists than the England of Charles I and Laud, but understanding what use these connections were to Clarke in his political mission requires some extrapolation. Most important, several lines of affinity emerge from his career in New England. In Newport, Clarke had, of course, known Obadiah Holmes as well as Mark Lucar. Lucar had been a member of John Spilsbury's church, and Holmes addresses his letter to William Kiffin and Spilsbury, who were among the leading London Baptists.[43]

Before forming his own congregation, William Kiffin was a member of Henry Jessey's church from 1638 until 1644.[44] Jessey led the most direct descendant of Henry Jacobs's independent church, which was a nursery of separate churches.[45] Jessey enjoyed what Murray Tolmie calls "a wide range of contacts among influential and radical puritans," including an earlier association with the Winthrop family.[46]

In the context of Clarke's suit, Jessey's most important association was with Hanserd Knollys. Knollys led a Baptist church in London starting in 1645, and he subscribed to the 1646 Confession, but not that of 1644. In June 1645, he baptized Jessey. Unlike most English Baptists, Knollys had direct experience of Massachusetts's intransigence. Fleeing Laudian persecution in 1636, he came to Boston, only to discover that "the Magistrates were told that I was an Antinomian, and desired that they would not suffer me to abide in their Patent."[47] Knollys passed a troubled four years as minister at "Piscattuah" (Portsmouth) in New Hampshire, before returning to England in 1641 as this part of New Hampshire came under the control of Massachusetts.[48] Just as Vane was in a political context, one imagines that Knollys was ready to testify as a harassed minister of the Gospel to the ambitions for territorial expansion and ideological hegemony cherished by the Bay Colony.

The other facet of Knollys's importance in Clarke's access to powerful auditors comes in his long association with John Wheelwright. Wheelwright was second only to Anne Hutchinson in the Antinomian movement: He had also suffered for the Bay Colony's efforts to silence dissent on its northern frontier, being forced out of Exeter, the town he founded, when that part of New Hampshire came into the orbit of the Bay Colony. He also was the preacher who by Knollys's own account, "opened to me the nature of the covenant of Free Grace," after his prayer was answered with the call "Go to Mr. Wheelwright."[49] Like Knollys, Wheelwright chose not to live as a dissenting preacher forced to stay one step ahead of the Bay Colony's encroachment, and returned to England. As an old friend and classmate of Cromwell's, Wheelwright enjoyed the favor of his government until the Restoration, when he returned to New England.[50]

There is also more direct evidence of Clarke's stature as a religious figure in Cromwell's London. On 3 August 1655, the Council of State directed that

> John Clarke, physician of Rhode Island in America, having composed and very closely compacted a new concordance to the Holy Scriptures of Truth, which, in regard to its plainness and fullness . . . may prove singularly conducive to the help of those who desire to try all things in these trying times by that touchstone of truth, Henry Hill[s] is licensed to print and publish the same.[51]

Unfortunately, the concordance does not survive, if it was published; more likely, other more urgent projects intervened for Henry Hills, who was one of the official printers to the Council of State and also the printer of *Ill Newes*.[52] Clarke's movements in England are hard to trace, and become more obscure in the second half of the 1650s, but at this juncture, Clarke enjoys enough prestige to be authorized to publish an important and quasi-official religious text. In the latter half of the 1650s, there is some evidence to suggest that this John Clarke was the one whose name appears on several Fifth Monarchist manifestoes, but this involvement, if it is by the same man, comes after he has performed his most important services on behalf of Aquidneck.[53]

Outside this religious context, the most important figure connecting Clarke to structures of power in London is Roger Williams. The two came together to England on the same errand, and it would only make sense for Williams to introduce Clarke to his own powerful associates. Foremost among these figures was Henry Vane the younger, who had been a governor of the Bay Colony during the Antinomian tumult and had left because of his dismay at the steps the colony took to suppress the Antinomians and because of his own political defeat. Vane was Williams's host for some of his stay in London, and, one imagines, predisposed to be sympathetic to those of Aquidneck who had been displaced by this crisis as he had been.[54]

Williams, of course, was also associated with John Milton on this visit, sharing his knowledge of Dutch in exchange for help with classical languages.[55] Milton, in his turn, was also in sympathy with Vane; he wrote a sonnet to him in July 1652. At this time, Milton was employed by Cromwell's government as Secretary for Foreign Tongues, and he enjoyed access to and influence with Cromwell.

These religious and civil networks are neither mutually exclusive nor by any means exhaustive, but are traced here to show how Clarke's message could find both sympathetic and influential auditors in England. The success of Clarke's campaign appears in two forms: support of Rhode Island and Providence Plantations, as well as rebukes of the Massachusetts Bay Colony.

The most dramatic evidence that the message of *Ill Newes* found sympathetic auditors in London comes in a letter Richard Saltonstall directed to John Cotton and John Wilson, the ministers of the Boston church. Responding to Clarke's reports of the behavior of the Bay Colony, he writes them:

> Reverend and Deare friends, whom I unfaynedly love and respect,
>
> It doth not a little grieve my spirit to heare what sadd things are reported dayly of your tyranny and persecutions in New-England, that you fyne, whip, and imprison men for their consciences.[56]

As the salutation indicates, this rebuke did not come from a Presbyterian or sectarian with little cause for sympathy to Massachusetts, but from one of the very founders of the Bay Colony itself. Sir Richard Saltonstall (1586–1661) was involved in the settlement from its embryonic state in England, pledging £100 in 1628 to the forerunner of the Massachusetts Bay Company.[57] Saltonstall sailed with Winthrop's party on the *Arabella*; his name appears as one of the signers of the *Humble Request*, the statement that the leaders of the settlement issued from the *Arabella* at Yarmouth.[58] He soon returned to England, but he remained a loyal supporter of the mission, defending it against the effort to recall the charter by *quo warranto* in 1635.[59] That he directs such sharp criticism to two of the leading ministers in Massachusetts not only suggests his own dismay at this turn of events but also suggests that he was trying to suggest to the men how opinion stood on the matter in England.

The shape of Saltonstall's criticism echoes the structure of Clarke's narrative, He chides the magistrates specifically for fining, whipping, and imprisoning men for their consciences—these are the three punishments

Clarke's party suffered. As Saltonstall refines his criticism, the major point he makes is that "you compell such to come into your assemblyes as you know will not joyne with you in your worship, and when they shew their dislike therof or witness against it, then you stirre up your magistrates to punish them for such (as you conceyve) are publike affronts."[60] As Clarke recounts it, this is exactly what happened to his contingent at Lynn. That a veritable "builder of the Bay Colony" takes the word, and the words, of a dissident, and hurls them across the ocean at two of the pillars of the church in New England gives a profound indication that Clarke's narrative found sympathetic readers beyond the circle of his friends and co-religionists.[61]

More important than the order licensing his concordance from Cromwell's government, or Saltonstall's rebuke of Cotton on the strength of his representations, was the outcome of the errand that had brought Clarke to England in the first place. In this errand, as in his later suit for a charter from Charles II, Clarke managed to prevail. Clarke and Williams arrived in England sometime before 30 March 1652, which is when Thomason dates Williams's *Fourth Paper, Presented by Major Butler.* On 8 April of that year, the Council of State refers the "petition of the free purchasers of the inhabitants of Rhode Island and Providence Plantations to the Committee for Foreign Affairs, to examine the matter of fact."[62] *Ill Newes* appeared shortly thereafter, on 15 May, and before any government body took up the suit in earnest, which suggests that Clarke composed or at least revised the text in London. A letter from Roger Williams to his brother dated 1 May indicates that several influential M.P.s, as well as Edward Winslow, appeared against the Clarke–Williams petition. The presence of Winslow against the petition demonstrates the continuing interest of the United Colonies in the preservation of Coddington's commission, but despite the support of Sir Arthur Hasselrig and George Fenwick, Cornelius Holland was able to stall proceedings until his patron Vane returned to London.[63] On 29 September 1652, the Council of State referred "the business concerning Rhode Island" to the Committee for Foreign Affairs.[64] On 2 October 1652, the council of State vindicated Clarke, effectively annulling the Coddington Charter: "The council have been informed that Mr. Coddington, sent from hence Governor of Rhode Island hath so behaved himself as hath produced great matters of complaint against him, now depending before us."[65] The order represents the immediate threat as coming from the Dutch, a more politic reason to provide than internecine threats, but the effect is to empower the "Magistrates and Free

Inhabitants of Providence Plantation . . . until further direction . . . for settling that Colony . . . to take care for the peace and quiet thereof." To this end, the Council of State gives the inhabitants of the colony broad powers to take Dutch ships at sea, and to defend itself against the "Dutch, or other enemies of this Commonwealth."[66] The effect of this order is to remove Coddington from power, and to continue the government under the provisions of the 1644 charter.

This vindication is more telling than it might seem. The language is typical of such instruments, in that it indicates that it is a temporary resolution until this committee can come to a better determination of the state of affairs. Such indecisive language, however, was the norm in the discourse of seventeenth-century colonial governance; a better determination was rarely possible, and the temporary solution could take the force of law for years on end. More important, while the language suggests an extension of the status quo for the time being, it is the *status quo ante* as established by the Long Parliament's Committee for Foreign Plantations for Clarke and Williams's plea, not the status quo created by Cromwell's Council of State with its grant to Coddington eighteen months previously.

This tendency to use temporizing language to regulate colonies persists in Cromwell's letter of 1655, which was in fact the final pronouncement of any Interregnum government on the disposition of Rhode Island. It is a more emphatic confirmation of the Williams charter than the 1652 order from the Council of State:

> Your agent here hath presented unto us some particulars concerning your Government, which you judge necessary to be settled by us here. But by reason of other great and weighty affairs of this Commonwealth, we have been necessitated to defer the consideration of them to a further opportunity . . . . In the mean time, we were willing to let you know, that you are to proceed in your Government according to the tenor of your Charter formerly granted on that behalf.[67]

Like the Council of State before him, Cromwell favored the construction of a 1644 Parliamentary committee over an order of his own Council of State in 1651.

What is striking about the success of this phase of Clarke's campaign for Rhode Island's autonomy is the facility with which he turned liabilities into assets for his cause. He was a member of a persecuted sect, inhabiting a corner of New England populated by exiles from the most powerful

English colony in America. And yet, with the example of Williams's and Gorton's victories over a stronger foe, and with his own keen ear for the discourse of suffering, Clarke was able to offer a narrative of New England that revised English understandings of the relations between Puritans and Antinomians and between Rhode Island and Massachusetts. Through his, John Crandall's, and Obadiah Holmes's deliberate engagement with the Bay Colony's judicial apparatus, Clarke was able to create a narrative that consciously employed the discourse of suffering to cast a colonial crisis in terms a metropolitan reader could grasp. John Clarke's travails as an Anabaptist made Aquidneck safe for Antinomians.

5. SUFFERING AND SUBSCRIBING

Configurations of Authorship
in the Quaker Atlantic

In the late 1650s and early 1660s, Quakers suffered in New England and published in England, just as Clarke and Gorton had before them. Publishing Quaker sufferings, however, was a far more elaborate proposition. Quaker apologists in New England, Barbados, and London worked in concert to publicize persecutions of Quakers, producing a distinctive, circum-Atlantic propaganda network. This discursive formation allowed Quaker apologists throughout the Atlantic world to make significant interventions on behalf of their oppressed brethren in New England, culminating in Charles II's 1661 order forbidding further Quaker executions by the Massachusetts Bay Colony.

Compared with earlier narratives of persecution coming out of New England, the most important feature of these Quaker narratives is the sheer quantity of them. In contrast to the individuated first-person narratives published by Gorton or John Clarke, the actual number of cases of Quaker persecution was dwarfed by ever-proliferating accounts of the same few events.

Despite their proliferation, one Quaker narrative of persecution does not duplicate the effort of another. Rather, taken as a whole, this literature is remarkably integrated. For instance, Humphrey Norton's *New-England's Ensigne* (1659) announces itself as a confirmation of an earlier text, Francis Howgill's *Popish Inquisition* (1659).[1] Norton's own travails in New England appear in Howgill's narrative; his own detailed narrative supports Howgill's London polemic. The Atlantic Ocean was more than body of water separating Friends from each other. In fact, the very distance between Old and New England afforded Quakers on both sides of the ocean unique discursive opportunities and effective ways to declare their dissent, while Barbados offered an outpost on the western rim of the Atlantic where Quakers could compile accounts of colonial suffering.

Quaker narratives of suffering use this Atlantic context to reconfigure authorship. Quaker tracts associate authorship more with the experience of suffering than with the physical processes of writing and publishing traditionally identified as the author's role. In many cases, texts are essentially authored by the suffering of the subject in the text—the name identified with the text is the sufferer, not the often anonymous person bringing the narrative to press. One Quaker suffers, and another "subscribes," or records and disseminates the experience. Quaker texts disassociate physical New World presence and experience from the act of writing and publishing these texts. The ocean intervenes, and those who suffer are not those who publish.

This model blurs the line between genre and author—identifying as a Quaker trumps individual identities. This diffuse structure also challenges the more individuated model of authorship in the modern world developed in the work of Michel Foucault and Roger Chartier. Foucault points to penal responsibility and proprietary rights as the foundation of what he calls the "author function." He asserts, "Books began to have authors . . . to the extent that authors became subject to punishment, that is to the extent that discourses could be transgressive."[2] Quaker narratives of suffering were transgressive, but neither penal responsibility nor proprietary claims (narratives of Quaker sufferings borrow extensively from one another) work to construct the familiar form of a modern, individuated author for these texts. Indeed, the fluid nature of Quaker authorial identity appears to be a product of inhabiting a space between penal responsibility and proprietary claims.[3] This fluidity is both literal and figurative—while bibliographers list *New-England's Ensigne* under Humphrey Norton's name, the work asserts that it is "Written at Sea, by us whom the wicked in scorn calls Quakers."[4] Ultimately, the quantity, cohesion, and diffusion of authorship create a medium for narrating sufferings that integrates colonies and metropolis into a network for reporting and publicizing the sufferings of Friends: the Quaker Atlantic. This discursive formation has ramifications outside the denominational history of the Quakers. Frederick Tolles and Kate Peters have both demonstrated how important print culture was to the development of the Society of Friends, but neither considers the role the Atlantic plays in much detail.[5] Peters gives a clear sense of the nature of Quaker print culture, but her chronological focus predates Quaker activity in New England. However, the Quaker movement she delineates, one that deploys print in a coordinated and sophisticated engagement with political affairs from its inception, suggests the foundation for the Quaker print campaign that took place on an Atlantic, rather than national, scale in the ensuing years.[6]

Quaker narratives of persecution belong both to Quaker print culture and Atlantic print culture, but neither of these in itself suffices to explain the distinct phenomenon of the Quaker narratives of New England sufferings that appeared in London from 1659 to 1661. The Atlantic allowed the dissemination and consumption of literature, but it also fostered new forms of literature. In crossing and recrossing the Atlantic, Quakers and their texts forged new relationships between experience and authorship, and authorship and publication.

I: The Quaker Invasion

The story of Quaker sufferings in Massachusetts is simple enough. The Quaker presence in New England began in 1656 with the arrival of Mary Fisher and Anne Austin from Barbados. It was not long before they were prosecuted for their faith, setting in motion a chain of events that would be repeated again and again over the next decade: Quakers come to Massachusetts, Massachusetts persecutes Quakers, Quakers narrate persecution and circulate these stories throughout the Atlantic world. Moreover, Quakers initiated this cycle in Plymouth, New Haven, and Connecticut as well. The same Quaker could suffer the same persecution in more than one jurisdiction and thus multiply the experiences of suffering that Quaker apologists could produce. Some of the more vigorous witnesses for the faith had what amounted to an itinerant prison ministry, with the variation that getting thrown in prison was central to the ministry. As Carla Pestana observes, "Quakers . . . were bent on confronting authority . . . . They refused to recognize the hegemony of the New England Way, recognition the authorities took for granted. In the Quaker invasion of Massachusetts, an immovable orthodoxy met the irresistible force of religious enthusiasm, with fatal results."[7] Specifically, the Bay Colony hanged four of its fellow English subjects on Boston Common: William Robinson and Marmaduke Stephenson in October 1659, Mary Dyer in June 1660, and William Leddra in March 1660/1.[8]

The thought of inflicting capital punishment on members of a sect now synonymous with pacifism is appalling, but in the context of the era, it is not remarkable that Massachusetts killed so many Quakers, but that they killed so few. By disseminating accounts of these proceedings, Quakers persuaded a newly restored Charles II to issue a writ of mandamus on 9 September 1661, which prohibited further executions by the Massachusetts Bay Colony.

Quaker narratives of persecution for this period define their experience in New England to such a degree that it is impossible to divorce the early history of the Quakers in New England from the sufferings they endured. While the persecution of other dissidents was limited in both intensity and duration, the early history of Quakers in New England was one of consistent and intense persecution, and persisted after the writ of mandamus forbade capital punishment under such Bay Colony innovations as the Cart and Whip Act.

It is important to recognize that the victims of these persecutions were not a few unfortunates who happened to run afoul of Bay Colony authorities. In the cases of Marmaduke Stephenson, William Robinson, William Leddra, and Mary Dyer, who lost their lives, not to mention Christopher Holder, John Copeland, and John Rous, who lost ears, as well as many others, there is a deliberate, willful, and repeated engagement by Quakers with the Bay Colony's legal apparatus.

The Quaker literature of persecution in New England falls into two distinct phases. In 1659 and 1660, Quakers detailed their corporal suffering, especially the ear-cutting of Copeland, Holder, and Rous. The executions of Quakers in Massachusetts from 1659 to 1661 inaugurated a surge in martyrologies in the early 1660s. Massachusetts continued to persecute Quakers after the writ of mandamus, but the narratives of the late 1660s and beyond, published after the writ of mandamus, such as Samuel Groome's *A Glass for the People of New England* (1676), are largely retrospectives of the intense sufferings occurring just before and just after the Restoration. The genre of the retrospective omnibus of Quaker persecution reached its zenith with Joseph Besse's *Collection of the Sufferings of the People Called Quakers* (1753). John Knott notes, "Besse's two folio volumes constitute what amounts to a Quaker version of Foxe's *Acts and Monuments.*"[9]

However, in 1659 and early 1660, Quakers began in earnest to produce accounts of their sufferings in New England without the distance from these events that Besse enjoyed. Francis Howgill's *Popish Inquisition* (1659), Humphrey Norton's *New-England's Ensigne* (1659), John Rous's

New-England a Degenerate Plant (1659), George Fox and John Rous's *The Secret Works of A Cruel People Made Manifest* (1659), and Joseph Nicholson's *The Standard of the Lord Lifted up in New-England* (1660) are pre-martyrdom narratives of persecution that constitute an important stage in the evolution of this form of dissent. Quakers are able to develop a credible literature of persecution, even before any of their brethren die in New England.

II: Lend Me Your Ear, and I'll Sing You a Song

A literature of persecution that does not require martyrdom of its protagonists has obvious appeal to its protagonists, but makes distinct demands on its narrators, because it allows narratives from sufferers themselves, rather than posthumous accounts from martyrologists. For an English reader in the middle of the seventeenth century, narratives of martyrdom would have been a familiar genre because of the enormous influence of Foxe's Book of Martyrs[10] John Knott links the Quaker interest in compiling sufferings to Foxe's influence. To adapt the conventions of Foxe's narratives of martyrdom to corporal, rather than capital, sufferings creates distinct challenges and opportunities for the author. The act of suffering does not silence the witness, but neither does it offer the kind of familiar script provided by the reiteration of martyr stories in Foxe.

There is another critical difference between Foxe's project and the Quaker effort to chronicle their sufferings in New England. Unlike Foxe or Besse, Quaker polemicists were working with immediate and contingent events. What emerges out of this intersection of generic tradition and historical circumstance is a series of narratives that present much more diffuse relationships between experience and authorship, or suffering and subscribing. The texts exist in London bookstalls, but not in the familiar form established by Foxe, where a distinct authorial figure gives identity to the experiences of martyrs.[11]

The relationship between suffering and authorship is vexed. Elaine Scarry, in her widely influential *The Body in Pain*, posits a distinct relationship between torture and language. She describes the process of torture as a process of "unmaking": Pain literally makes the objects in the prisoner's world disappear, replacing them with only pain. Thus, if a prisoner provides information under the interrogation that is usually (though not as consistently as Scarry suggests) part of torture, this is not an act of "betrayal," because the world the prisoner's words identify has ceased to exist for him or her. Thus, for Scarry, a principal outcome of torture is its ability to destroy language.[12]

Scarry's examples come primarily from various despotic regimes of the Cold War era, especially in Greece and South America, but she frames her argument in terms of universals determined by basic human physiology. Janel Mueller, while recognizing the impact of Scarry's work, elaborates a case that demonstrates a rather different paradigm for the relation between bodies, torture, and making. In examples from Foxe's Book of Martyrs, she demonstrates that torture, in this case the burning of Protestant martyrs by Marian inquisitors, in fact furnished dramatic examples of self-making in the flames. Mueller quotes Foxe's account of the death of John Hooper:

> "And these ['Lord Jesus, receive my spirit'] were the last words he was heard to utter. But when he was black in the mouth, and his tongue swollen, that he could not speak . . . and he knocked his breast with his hands, until one of his arms fell off, and then knocked still with the other . . . and his hand did cleave fast to the iron upon his breast."

Of this scene, Mueller notes, "The capacity of Hooper's body to produce a significant gesture in its hour of destruction yields an affirmative demonstration of torture's failure to unmake a self."[13]

In the context of early modern England, Mueller's objection to the sweep of Scarry's argument seems well founded. However, it is worth remembering that the narrative we have of this event comes from Foxe. Thus, it might be more precise to say that *as Foxe narrates it*, the capacity of Hooper's body to produce a significant gesture in its hour of destruction yields an affirmative demonstration of torture's failure to prevent a martyr from contributing to a Protestant hagiography.

Hooper's gesture and Foxe's litany of other scenes of stoicism in the flames are hard not to read as having as much to do with mythology as with history. However, Foxe is not a journalist, and he does not generally have to contend with competing unsympathetic eyewitness accounts. In a later American context, our temporal separation from the moment of Nathan Hale's execution renders his appropriation of "I regret that I have but one life to lose for my country" from Addison's *Cato* as he faces the scaffold simultaneously indisputable and mythological. One imagines that a Tory newspaper reporting the event at the time would follow a different script.

What the accession of Elizabeth does for Foxe, the ocean does for Quakers. Spatial, rather than historical, distance affords the same opportunity for mythmaking, and even in the corporal phase of their sufferings, Quakers make ready use of Foxe's scaffold mythologies. Beyond their distance from London, other factors make these Quaker persecutions distinct. We would certainly recognize ear-cutting as barbaric, as cruel and unusual, but it is not torture integrated with interrogation in the sense Scarry describes.[14] Considered as a discursive gesture, interrogative torture asks its victims questions: "Who are your accomplices?" "Where is the bomb?" These questions may be a pretext, but they give the event of torture its structure. At the same time, systematic degradation and pain, like that perpetrated at Abu Ghraib prison after the invasion of Iraq, seems more intended to gratify the perverse whims of the perpetrators than to serve any interest of the state. Cases like Copeland, Holder, and Rous seem to fall in between. This is punishment-as-spectacle, a declaration from judicial power of judicial power. The actual event is brief, but its result is permanent, and the disfiguration of the victim reveals his or her transgression, as well as the power of the state.[15]

London Quaker pamphleteer Francis Howgill was the first to challenge this power. He was an early and energetic Quaker adherent, to the degree that he attempted to convert Oliver Cromwell in 1653.[16] He was active throughout the later 1650s as a Quaker apologist, and this experience defending his faith in print made him an ideal candidate to relate the woes of the New England Quakers, even though he never visited North America at all.

That Howgill would be the first Quaker to condemn the practices of the Bay Colony indicates a degree of cooperation among the Quakers involved. Not only would it have been necessary for Quakers returning from New England to provide Howgill with the details of their sufferings, but they would also have to restrain themselves from offering competing accounts of their own experience to sympathetic Quaker printers and booksellers. Even in this first Quaker narrative of suffering, the question of authorship is problematic.

The text of *Popish Inquisition* indicates that Howgill's fellows were wise in their decision to leave the field to him. Howgill made a specialty of responding to anti-Quaker pamphlets in the 1650s, and this text is one that

demonstrates his considerable facility in crafting polemic. Not surprisingly, Howgill turns to the familiar images of Revelation to characterize his
adversary as "the beast who rose out of the sea, to kill with the sword all
that worshipped him not."[17] Thus, Howgill introduces his work with "In
the ensuing discourse, thou wilt see great Professors, [of] the Churches of
New-England . . . making war for their Mother, Mystery Babylon."[18]

In this preface, Howgill also explicitly delineates his role as the compil-
er of this narrative: "The Narrative of the Sufferings is some of them from
men of their own Nation, the rest is the Sufferers own Narration . . . the
substance of which I extracted for the Readers sake."[19] The focus of *Popish Inquisition* is on the sufferings of Christopher Holder, John Rous, and
John Copeland. Along with others, Holder and Copeland were arrested at
Boston in November 1657, where they and John Rous eventually lose an
ear apiece.

Holder, Rous, and Copeland made quite a business of vexing the Bay
Colony, for it was only after repeated offenses that they each faced the
penalty of losing an ear for their incursions. Even from this threatened
position, they challenge the dignity and legitimacy of their captors, asking, "We have seen some of your laws that have many Scriptures in the
Margent, but what example have you in Scripture for cutting off ears?"[20]
In relating the communication from the Boston prisoners, Howgill takes
pains to describe the ear-cutting as a gross departure from the norms of
English justice: "We seeing their unjust proceedings against us, and that
they were both our Accusers and Judges, we were stirred in Spirit to appeal to the chief Magistrate of the Commonwealth of England . . . but they
made a light thing of it, and hastened the Keeper to put us away." Upon
the scene of the actual execution of this sentence, the Boston prisoners
seek the traditional staging of their suffering, and are denied: "Christoph.
Holder said, Such Execution as this should be done publikely, and not in
private. One called Cap. Oliver, replyed, We do it in private, to keep you
from twatling."[21]

On several levels, this representation of the Bay Colony's procedure
works to elicit the sympathies of Quaker and non-Quaker alike. Despite
whatever an English reader might think about the faith and practice of
the Quakers, this description of the Bay Colony's practice shows an ille-
gitimate entity usurping the power and authority of English law to abuse
an English subject. As Howgill presents this scene, it is not necessary to
sympathize with Quakers to recognize the enormities of the Bay Colony's
injustice. The exchange between Holder and Captain Oliver about the

venue of their ear-cutting extends this notion of Massachusetts perver-
sions of English justice. Staging executions and punishment in public was
an English custom with deep roots in the culture: On the one hand, it
served to open these actions to public scrutiny; on the other, the execution or punishment was a site in the culture that afforded the public with
a spectacle and the condemned with a forum. Here, Holder's appeal for
a public enactment of his punishment seems to be founded as much on a
sense of custom as of legal precedent. It is not hard to imagine gathering
to witness public punishment among the communal and social activities
like "church ales, whitsun processions, football, and maypole reveling"
that Philip Round identifies as a source of friction between Puritanism
and early modern English popular culture.[22]

The Bay Colony's decision to conceal this act of mutilation is curious.
Of capital punishments, Foucault observes, "The public execution did
not re-establish justice; it reactivated power. In the seventeenth century,
and even in the early eighteenth century, it was not, therefore, with all
its theatre of terror, a lingering hang-over from an earlier age." Colonial
corporal mutilation is different from metropolitan capital execution, but
both would seem to fit with what Foucault calls "the liturgy of torture
and execution—above all, the importance of a ritual that was to deploy its
pomp in public. Nothing was to be hidden of this triumph of the law."[23]
The magistrates' reluctance to carry out this punishment in public may
be due to their awareness of another aspect of punishment-as-spectacle.
The more elaborate the spectacle, the greater is the chance that the meaning of the performance can be inverted and redound to the credit of the
prisoner and the shame of the executioners. Foucault famously describes
such a scene at the opening of *Discipline and Punish* with the execution
of Damiens: "The executioner . . . took the steel pincers which had been
specially made for the occasion, and which were about a foot and a half
long, and pulled first at the calf of the right leg . . . the executioner found
it so difficult to tear away pieces of flesh that he set about the same spot
two or three times . . . and what he took away formed at each part a wound
about the size of a six-pound crown piece." Justice fares little better when
it attempts to quarter Damiens: "The horses tugged hard, each pulling
straight on a limb . . . . After a quarter of an hour, the same ceremony was
repeated, and after several attempts, the direction of the horses had to be
changed . . . without success." Ultimately, the executioner has to facilitate
the process by cutting through Damiens' joints with a pocket knife; this
brutal enactment of state power disintegrates into an embarrassing fiasco.

As Foucault observes, "in punishment-as-spectacle a confused horror spread from the scaffold . . . it was always ready to invert the shame inflicted on the victim into pity or glory, [and] it often turned the legal violence of the executioner into shame."[24]

The Bay Colony, perhaps fearing this sort of scene, chooses to cut ears away from the public square. In the narrative, however, the actual public or private venue is irrelevant, for the story will inhabit the public venue of print. Thus, the victims disdain to describe the moment of the fulfillment of this punishment, or the pain it entails, but rather reiterate the shameful bearing of their oppressors: "So when they had done, they slank away as a Dog when he had suck'd the blood of a Lamb, and is discovered."[25] Despite the secret, inquisitorial nature of these proceedings, they produce the same kind of contagion of dissent that Baptist Obadiah Holmes's public whipping in Boston had produced early in the decade, where public punishment attracted witnesses to the cause of the prisoner: "The Friend that came to bear witness against their cruelty (whose Name is Katherin Scott) is committed to the House of Correction."[26]

The author of much of the remainder of *Popish Inquisition* is the Massachusetts Bay Colony. Howgill reprints a law against Quakers, and letters from Bay Colony magistrates John Endicott and Richard Bellingham. A distinctive aspect of Howgill's attacks on the Bay Colony is his ability to identify them with a specific and palpable evil, as in his connection of the ministers and magistrates to the whore and beast of Revelation, "deceived with the Wine of the Fornication of the Whore."[27] In introducing the material he reproduces from Bay Colony laws, he identifies them specifically as the work of the Devil: "And now the Devil being let loose for a little season, he rages, and goes into utter darkness . . . that so none but he, may have any rule in the Town of Boston . . . . The last piece of Work which the rules have done for their master is as followeth."[28]

In tarring his opponents with this infernal brush, Howgill does more than insult their faith and honor. In essence, the image of these laws as an execution of the Devil's will is Howgill's way of trumping the language of the law itself. The law specifies that Quakers are a "pernicious sect" maintaining "dangerous and horrid Tenents," and continues in this vein.[29] Howgill's reproduction of the law never continues for long before he interrupts with a rejoinder much longer than the portion of the law he has just presented. Like narratives of trials produced by the accused, this technique creates a voice capable of interrupting the Bay Colony's monologue of justice in print even when it cannot speak in court. As Peters observes of an earlier generation of debate, "Quaker authors regarded printed exchanges between themselves and their critics as primarily instrumental for spreading the truth and increasing the following of the Quaker movement: they did not debate with puritan adversaries as a matter of principle, or for the sake of it."[30]

Popish Inquisition asserts the burgeoning power and authority of Quaker discourse. The discursive network Bellingham and Endicott seek to establish to record the sins of the Quakers is taken over by Howgill and used to defend this same faith. For Howgill, the offshore persecutions of Quakers are useful to his larger cause, in that he can dare to speak more freely against Quaker persecution abroad than against domestic persecutions. This entire document is a testament to the powerful coordination of Quakers on both sides of the Atlantic. Howgill arranges and marshals material from a variety of sources into a coherent expression of the injustices Quakers face in New England, a discourse that, at the same time, offers an implicit criticism of the treatment of Quakers in England.

Evidence of this coordination is visible by comparison of *Popish Inquisition* with the other major narrative of Quaker suffering from the pre-execution period, Humphrey Norton's *New-England's Ensigne*. On its title page is an endorsement that "This being a confirmation of so much as Francis Howgill has truly published in his Book titled, The Popish Inquisition."[31] The experienced pamphleteer Howgill rushed an account into print, followed by the more extensive eyewitness account from Norton. In addition, the reference from the one text to the other tends to knit them into a mutually reinforcing network of truth, more credible than isolated tracts on similar topics.

In many respects, *New-England's Ensigne* is a confirmation of Howgill's text, just as Norton claims, and thus it recapitulates much of Howgill's content. In some respects, though, Norton offers variations on Howgill's text and has more documentary material at hand. In particular, Norton offers detailed accounts of New England laws against Quakers, and documents from specific legal proceedings against Quakers. Frequently, but not always, these laws are set in Gothic type, giving them a menacing aspect next to the Roman type of the narrative.[32] George Bishop's *New England Judged by the Spirit of the Lord* used a similar typographic technique.

Norton does not have Howgill's polemical gifts, but his narrative does have the attestation of personal witness, and, indeed, Norton offers an extensive section in his preface asserting the truth of the words that follow. This testimony is presented in the context of a brief account of his path

and kept Priſoners by the Conſtables Deputie ; who being de-
manded a copie of the Warrant, a friend that ſtood by ſaid it
was a uſual thing to give a Copie of it, if required, was after-
ward for ſo ſaying fined 10 ſhillings ; when to *Plymouth* we
were brought, where was then ſitting the Magiſtrates hereafter named, we ſtanding before them, the power of the Lord
being over them, they ſaid little to us, only told us of a Law
that they had whereby we were not to ſtay in their Colony ; we
required to ſee it, they anſwered, it was ſufficient that they
ſaid it, and would not ſhew it to us ; ſo after ſaying that they
did beleeve that we did not know that they had ſuch a law, yet
required us to depart, the which thing we could not do ; they
proceeded to ſentence us, threatning of us if we came again ,
they would exerciſe the Law on us which is for Vagabonds : So
they ſtill kept us Priſoners committing us into the Conſtables
hand, and wrote a Warrant, a true Copie is as followeth :

   New Plymouth *to the under-Marſhal of the Juriſdiction of*
     Plymouth *aforeſaid.*

   𝔚hereas there hath been two extravagant perſons profeſſ-
ing themſelves to be 𝔔uakers at the 𝔗own of Plymouth ,
who according to order may not be permitted to abide within the
liberty of our juriſdiction. 𝔗heſe are therefore in the 𝔑ame of
his Highneſs the 𝔏ord 𝔓rotector of England, Scotland and Ireland, to will and command you forthwith on Receit hereof, to
convoy the ſaid perſons, *viz.* Chiſtopher Holder and John Copeland, unto the utmoſt bounds of our Juriſdiction : 𝔚hereof fail
not at your peril :

Dated at Plymouth the	Thomas Prince Governour.
31 of Auguſt, 57.	John Alden.
	Joſiah Winſlow.
	Thomas Southworth.

   The which Warrant was put in Execution by the under Mar-
ſhal on us, who did have us out of the Juriſdiction vvhich vvas
fifty miles to Road Iſland, ſo he left us on the ſecond of the ſe-
venth moneth, 1657. vve then going to it, and that none may
queſtion the truth which is here in ſhort related, we ſhall be ready to confirm it, who are true Witneſſes of it, whoſe Names are
here ſubſcribed,   *Chriſtopher Holder, John Copeland.*

                                                 Thus

FIGURE 7: From Humphrey Norton,
New Englands Ensigne (London: 1659).
*Courtesy of Houghton Library, Harvard College Library *AC6.N8243.659n.*

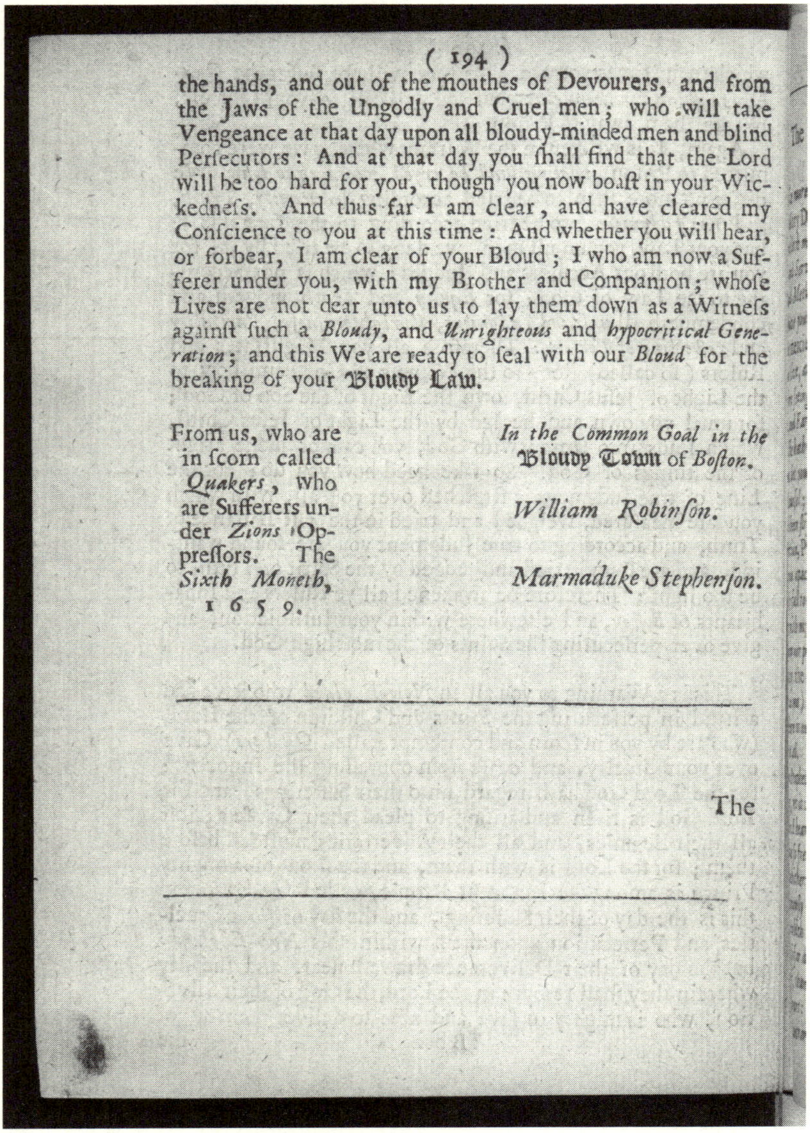

(194)

the hands, and out of the mouthes of Devourers, and from
the Jaws of the Ungodly and Cruel men; who will take
Vengeance at that day upon all bloudy-minded men and blind
Perſecutors : And at that day you ſhall find that the Lord
will be too hard for you, though you now boaſt in your Wic-
kedneſs. And thus far I am clear, and have cleared my
Conſcience to you at this time : And whether you will hear,
or forbear, I am clear of your Bloud ; I who am now a Sufferer under you, with my Brother and Companion; whoſe
Lives are not dear unto us to lay them down as a Witneſs
againſt ſuch a *Bloudy*, and *Unrighteous* and *hypocritical Generation*; and this We are ready to ſeal with our *Bloud* for the
breaking of your 𝕭loudy 𝕷aw.

From us, who are
in ſcorn called
Quakers, who
are Sufferers un-
der *Zions* Op-
preſſors. The
Sixth Moneth,
1 6 5 9.

In the Common Goal in the
𝕭loudy 𝕿own *of Boſton.*

William Robinſon.

Marmaduke Stephenſon.

The

FIGURE 8: From George Bishop,
New England Judged by the Spirit of the Lord (London: 1661).
*Courtesy of Houghton Library, Harvard College Library *EC65.B5416.661n.*

to his faith, offering some of the expression of spirituality absent from Howgill: "I was in darkness . . . then out of the belly of hell cryed I, so grievous was my complaint . . . then called I to question all that I had either read or heard . . . which set me to inquire after this new light."[33] This testimony of the Truth underwrites the truth of the narrative to follow: "and least thou or any one should question the truth hereof, we the Sufferers are the Subscribers, who are all of us by name and nature free-born English people."[34] As with many other similar tracts, Norton's name does not appear on the title page, but only appears appended to the portions he wrote, while what he compiled from others is subscribed by them, in that their names appear below text identified with them. Earlier narratives of persecution by the Bay Colony were narratives of individual victims like Samuel Gorton or John Clarke, and their narratives had single authors. Here it is a group that is persecuted, and it is a group that prepares the narrative.

Suffering and subscribing as a model for authorship shifts emphasis from acts of composition to facts of experience.[35] This formulation of authorship may explain why some Quakers in New England made a business of suffering: If the experience of suffering is required for the act of witness, it can serve faithful Quakers as a mandate to subject themselves to persecution. In Norton's case, he seems to pursue his "pursevants" more than they pursue him, running afoul of authorities in the three out of the four United Colonies during his brief sojourn in New England, and he seems to have done his best to add Connecticut to Plymouth, Massachusetts, and New Haven.

A minor, yet significant, rhetorical turn is Norton's use of the word "persevant" to describe a Plymouth magistrate, making an explicit connection to the bad old days of Laud that the citizens of Plymouth and Boston had themselves fled. With these references to the Laudian persecution, or elsewhere to the Marian terrors, the aim of Quaker pamphleteers is not to differentiate, but rather to connect themselves to the main stream of Protestant history. As Knott points out, with the systematic publication of sufferings, Quakers "reinforced their sense of themselves as belonging to the line of martyrs for God's truth."[36] Burrough compares the treatment of Mary Dyer on the scaffold to Bonner's predations, while George Bishop comments that Boston's abuses are worse than Bonner's were.[37] These Friends claim not just a tradition of martyrdom, but an explicitly Protestant tradition of martyrdom. It is the province of heresiographers to denounce the appearance of new sects as cataclysmic eruptions on the religious landscape, and the nature of sectarians to resist these formulations. Underhill described the rise of the Quakers as "Hell broke loose." In a similar vein, Mather characterized Gorton as "a prodigious minter of exhorbiant [sic] novelties."[38] In their apologies, however, the Quakers do not represent their faith as a novelty, appearing ex nihilo, but rather as the refined stream of a river otherwise grown brackish and turbid. As dismayed as they are with the faith of their contemporaries, here and elsewhere, the Quakers are not shy to claim their portion of an English Protestant legacy.

If anything, it is the Bay Colony that is increasingly portrayed as an apostate body. As Norton comments, introducing yet another litany of Massachusetts abuses, "And this they do because they neither know the Father nor us, they hate us without a cause."[39] In some places, Norton's closer proximity to the scene of the persecutions, and access to other manuscripts, allow him to improve on Howgill, as in an extended recreation of Holder, Copeland, and Rous's parley with the magistrates shortly before they each lost an ear. As Richard Bauman points out, such scenes are "social drama . . . it is apt to consider the trials [of Quakers] on the basis of a set of features they display in common with theatrical drama."[40] Indeed, the Quakers were not the first dissidents to recognize the theatrical potential of the court. Describing the literary figuration of the English reading public as a jury in John Lilburne's pamphlets, Sharon Achinstein notes "the proceedings 'pleased the public as well . . . as if they had acted before them one of Ben Jonson's plays,'" observing that "the courtroom provided a kind of entertainment sorely lacking after the closing of the theatres in 1641."[41] As in John Clarke's *Ill Newes*, these scenes give defendants the twofold advantage of being heard at all, and of having the opportunity to consider and polish their rejoinders for the press.

An extreme example of this conceit of judicial system as theater comes upon the execution of the sentence of Holder, Rous, and Copeland each to lose an ear. At the moment they suffer this punishment, they say together, "They that do it ignorantly we do desire from our hearts the Lord to forgive them, but them that do it maliciously, let our blood be upon their heads."[42] This is a pretty fancy speech to deliver just after losing an ear, but in its portrayal of superhuman forbearance upon the execution of a violent punishment, it is in keeping with Foxe's classic accounts of martyrdom, as when Cranmer steadfastly thrusts his hand into the flames, with his hand being consumed by the flames before they touch his body.

The account of the ear-cutting comes in a narrative that Norton says "came to my hands in Barbados," which points to the importance of Quaker mobility for producing these texts. Beyond Norton's extensive travel through New England, he also visits distant Friends in the Caribbean before returning to England. His experience seems to be the rule, rather than the exception, at least for prominent Quakers. Anne Austin and Mary Fisher come to New England by way of Barbados, and even George Fox, a founder of the faith, made a visit to New England.

The Quaker Atlantic was not simply defined by a metropolis and a colonial outpost separated by an ocean. Between the scaffolds in Boston and presses in London, Barbados and Rhode Island played critical roles in shaping the practice and discourse of Quaker suffering. Barbados was a frequent port of call for ships traveling between North America and England and, fortuitously, an early and robust Quaker outpost.[43] Experiences, manuscripts, and printed books could be exchanged among friends bound for other corners of the Atlantic world. To cite one specific example, the account of William Leddra's death that appears in *New England Judged* appears in the form of a letter to the master of a ship in port at Barbados.[44] If Barbados was a key Quaker entrepot, Rhode Island functioned to permit both terrestrial and marine mobility. After the Port Act prohibited Quakers from landing in Boston, landing in Rhode Island and proceeding overland allowed immediate access to three of the four New England Puritan colonies. In *A Declaration of the General Court . . . Concerning the Execution of two Quakers*, the Bay Colony describes this process: "accordingly a Law was made and published, prohibiting all Masters of Ships, to bring any Quaker into this Jurisdiction . . . Notwithstanding which, by a back Door, they found entrance."[45] In a domestic context, too, Rhode Island's tolerance was an important resource. Bordering Plymouth, Connecticut, and Massachusetts, the tiny colony offered a space where Quakers could rest and plan new excursions into hostile territory without fear of persecution. Being able to retreat to Rhode Island allowed Quakers to dictate the time and place of their encounters with the juridical systems of Rhode Island's less tolerant neighbors.

Against this mobility, the Quakers' opponents were rarely in a position to make informed rebuttals to their representations of their abuses. From time to time, Massachusetts dispatched agents, such as sending John Norton to offer *The Heart of New England Rent* as a rejoinder to the flood of Quaker pamphlets, but such projects were fundamentally reactive in nature, and rarely timely. Quakers could cross and recross the ocean and remain Friends, while Bay Colony representatives dispatched to England were prone to take up broader concerns of church and state and not return to New England, as in the case of Hugh Peter.

Humphrey Norton's mobility enables him to write effectively against New England's persecution. A product of his wide travel in New England as well as the Atlantic world, his narrative fuses the experience of suffering with an awareness of its contexts. Inhabiting a more fluid and cosmopolitan Atlantic world than their adversaries did, it was possible for Quakers to dominate the discourse about their persecutions abroad; in Old England or New a Quaker could find Friends, while New England could find few friends in Old England, and fewer still after the Restoration.

One of the most significant supporters of New England Quakers was, of course, George Fox, the founder and leader of the sect. In *The Secret Workes of a Cruel People Made Manifest* (1659), Fox covers the same ground as *Popish Inquisition* and *New-England's Ensigne*, but does not duplicate these efforts. Indeed, the three texts taken together suggest a nuanced sense of genre and audience for Quaker propaganda. Howgill's polemic injects the issue into public consciousness, Norton's account offers details for the edification of the brethren, and Fox's shorter account summarizes these texts in the context of a direct address to Parliament.

The increasing sophistication of the Quaker engagement with print culture also manifests itself here in a more material form. Fox concludes his pamphlet by reproducing a letter written by James Cudworth, a Plymouth magistrate, to a friend in England expressing unease about the persecution of Quakers. This same letter also appears in Rous's *New England a Degenerate Plant* (1659), a pamphlet reproducing New England's anti-Quaker laws for the edification of London readers. The typography, explanatory matter, and line breaks for this version are the same as in its other appearance, suggesting that the letter was set in type and appended to two different pamphlets in succession.

III: Quaker Acts and Monuments

In 1660, Quakers would need all of the advantages their mobility and sophistication could provide. In 1660, the cultural field for Quaker pamphlets changed in two important ways. First, Quakers now had stories of martyrdom to punctuate their narratives of persecution. Second, the ultimate audience for these appeals was now Charles II, the restored Stuart monarch. The ramifications of these two conditions were far from predictable. Charles II had more pressing concerns than the disposition of his New England colonies, but even so, it would be difficult for him to decide just who his friends were in New England. If their opponents could argue that the Quakers represented the spirit of radical religion that had characterized England during the Commonwealth and Protectorate, Quaker apologists could as easily suggest that the New England government still represented the crusading spirit of Puritanism of the 1630s and 1640s that had cost Charles I his head. This is a gross oversimplification of the situation the various New England colonies faced in 1660, but it does serve to illustrate that the government of Charles II did not have a clear allegiance to one party or the other in this ongoing struggle between Quakers and orthodox Puritans in New England. Thus, in this milieu, success becomes more a matter of persuasion, and despite their small numbers and marginal status, the Quakers were better placed, better informed, and better suited to craft an argument for the king's ear than were their rivals in Massachusetts.

Against this relatively fluid colonial situation, however, one must be mindful of the rigid domestic policies of the restored king. Despite the pledges of the Declaration of Breda, Charles II's administration worked quickly to suppress religious heterodoxy, banning conventicles on 10 January 1660/1, then passing a series of acts over the next four years to reestablish the Anglican Church, acts known collectively as the Clarendon Code. The question facing Quakers in 1660, then, was how to convince a king bent on enforcing religious conformity at home to guarantee protection from religious persecution abroad.

To this end, several narratives of Quaker sufferings appeared in London around the time of the restoration. At this pivotal moment, it is worth remembering that it is difficult to know just who in England was reading these narratives. The enemies of the Quakers refer to one another, rather than to Quaker propaganda; among moderate English citizens, a subtle shift in public opinion about the treatment of Quakers is difficult to trace from this remove. However, the evolution of these narratives of persecution indicates that one significant audience for the early Quaker narratives of persecution was other Quakers. From Howgill to Bishop, the narratives have an accretive quality, with the material of an earlier text incorporated into subsequent versions. Roughly speaking, in a parallel phenomenon, incidents of persecution follow a two-stage procedure in reaching the attention of interested London readers: Sufferers or their close associates prepare narratives describing various incidents of persecution, which are then compiled or reiterated by more prominent and influential English Quakers, including George Fox, Edward Burrough, and Isaac Pennington. For these writers, the audience of salient importance is the restored king and his advisers in a political context, and their brethren in a spiritual context.

Around the time of the restoration several new accounts of Quaker travails issued from London presses. Among them were Joseph Nicholson's *The Standard of the Lord Lifted up in New England* (1660), Marmaduke Stephenson's *Call from Death to Life* (1660), and George Bishop's *New England Judged by The Spirit of the Lord* (1661), which was the most extensive chronicle of early sufferings in New England. Humphrey Smith produced a 1660 broadside entitled "To New England's pretended Christians." The subject also engaged the attention of major figures among the English Quakers. In April 1660, Isaac Pennington published *An Examination of the Grounds or Causes, which are said to induce the Court of Boston . . . to make that Order . . . of Banishment . . . An answer to the True Relation of the Proceedings against Quakers*, an answer to an October 1659 appendix to John Norton's defense of the Bay Colony, while at the end of 1660 Edward Burrough offered *A Declaration of the sad and great Persecution and Martyrdom of the People of God, called Quakers, in New England, for the Worshipping of God.*

Marmaduke Stephenson and William Robinson's *A Call from Death to Life* is a classic of the genre. This is the first Quaker tract fully to grasp the possibilities of the suffering narrative as a spiritual resource for the faithful, as well as a political tool against skeptics.

A Call's authorial structure is unusually complex. The work is catalogued under Marmaduke Stephenson's name—this attribution is conventional, but problematic. Strictly speaking, the phrase "A Call From Death to Life" is attached to the prefatory spiritual narrative, not to the work as a whole, but the syntax of the title page illustrates this confusion, if it does not clarify it.

There is "A Call . . .," "written by Marmaduke Stephenson," then letters from Stephenson and Robinson, and finally, "the true copy of a letter as it came to our hands, from a Friend in New England." The title page uses the third person for Stephenson, the putative author, while identifying another presence, "our hands," as the agent ultimately responsible for the work in its printed manifestation. Evidently, these hands belong to the signatories of the introductory section titled "To the reader": John Whitehead, Marmaduke Storre, William Padley, Gregory Milner, and

A CALL

FROM

Death to Life,

AND

Out of the Dark wayes and Worships of the World where
the Seed is held in Bondage under the Merchants of
Babylon, Written by *Marmaduke Stephenſon*;

Who (together with another dear Servant of the Lord called
William Robinſon) hath (ſince the Writing hereof) ſuffer-
ed Death, for bearing Witneſſe to the ſame Truth,
amongſt the Profeſſors of *Boſtons* Juriſdiction
in *New England*.

With a True Copy of Two Letters, which they Writ to the Lords
People a little before their Death.

And alſo the True Copy of a Letter as it came to our hands, from
a Friend in *New England*, which gives a brief Relation of the
manner of their Martyrdom, with ſome of the Words which they
expreſt at the time of their ſuffering.

John 16. 2,3.

*They ſhall put you out of their Aſſemblies, yea the time cometh, that who-
ſoever killeth you, will think that he doth God ſervice; And theſe
things will they do unto you, becauſe they have not known the Father nor
Me, ſaith Chriſt.*

London, Printed for *Thomas Simmons*, at the Sign of the
Bull and Mouth near *Alderſgate*. 1660.

FIGURE 9: From title page, Marmaduke Stephenson,
A Call from Death to Life (London: 1660).
Courtesy of the John Carter Brown Library.

Thomas Leemin.[46] In obvious and practical ways, suffering death further complicates the authorship of these tracts. Beyond authorship, the title page also clouds the issue of just what work it identifies—"A Call from Death to Life" refers ambiguously to Stephenson's testimony, and to the entire publication.

To make matters more complex, while this narrative is identified with Stephenson and Robinson, they obviously were not responsible for compiling and publishing it. The ability and zeal of the Quakers to disseminate the last utterances of their martyrs posthumously was a critical factor in their campaign; death amplified, rather than silenced, the testimony of their martyrs.

Anticipating his posthumous audience, Stephenson specifically directs his opening missive to his "dear Neighbors and People in the Town of Shipton and Wighton."[47] What follows is not simply an account of his sufferings, but a moving account of the path of life that has brought him to his cell, with an emphasis on his conversion, coupled with an exhortation to his readers to find the Spirit within themselves, to "come buy wine and milk without mony and without price."[48]

Stephenson's concern is to edify his listeners about the peril to their souls, not to his body. Imprisonment provides an opportunity to preach and gives a double meaning to the title. While Stephenson's own words are the words of a dead man to his living brethren, the call he sounds is from death in sin to life in salvation: "the Lord in his Eternal Love and Pity to my Soul, hath redeemed me from my fallen estate, and raised my soul from Death to Life."[49] The letter that is the heart of this tract has nothing to say about Stephenson's persecution and execution; instead, it exists as a framing device, giving his testimony for his life in Christ gravity and prominence. An exhortation of this sort, one imagines, would be harder to ignore than one from a living witness to truth, and suggests that the Quakers who prepared this pamphlet were alive to the spiritual nourishment such stories could bring their adherents, along with the discredit they could bring their opponents.

This tender exhortation to faith takes up the bulk of the tract and is the heart of its spiritual substance. The compilers of this pamphlet do link this narrative with the larger Quaker struggle by including correspondence Stephenson and Robinson had with the Boston Court, and with Christopher Holder, another prominent Quaker victim of persecution, and by appending accounts of their sentencing and martyrdom. A key scene in these events comes in Robinson's account of his sentencing, when he "desired

that I might read a Paper to them and the people there present, which was
a declaration of my Call . . . John Indicott their Governour in a furious
manner said, I should not read it, neither would they hear it read . . . I said
I should leave the paper with them, which I did soon cast upon the Table
amongst them."[50] This "Call" echoes the call that Stephenson does offer
to his brethren at home, displaying the contrast between New England
and Old: The "Professors" in Boston restrain the discourse that circulates
freely among Friends in England. That these words cannot be uttered in
front of a court full of ministers and magistrates advertises the strength of
these words as much as the weakness of these officials.

Stephenson suffers the same sentence as Robinson, "to be hanged on
the Gallows, til you are dead."[51] Sentenced along with them is Mary Dyer,
who would become the most prominent of the Quaker martyrs in New
England. This is among the first mentions of her suffering, and her role in
this tract is marginal, but her association with the martyrdom of Stephenson and Robinson would become an important feature of her own story.

Stephenson and Robinson offer final letters of farewell and exhortation to their brethren, and a letter from Peter Pearson offers an account
of their actual martyrdom. Pearson, describing his task as delivering "tidings of heaviness and joy," writes from Plymouth Prison in December
1659. It is impossible to determine whether he offers an actual eyewitness
account, but certainly the narrative he sends to England is quite stylized.
Indeed, as Pearson describes the scene, it seems almost as though Robinson and Stephenson collaborate with their executioners in an elaborate
ritual. They speak, and the executioner's men hinder them, all the way up
the scaffold:

> W.R. spake these words, saying this is your hour, and the power
> of darknesse, then the Drummer beat up his drum . . . And when
> they were come to the Ladders foot, they took leave of each other,
> and W.R. stept up the Ladder and spake to the People, saying, this
> is the day of your visitation . . . as he spake, the executioner bound
> his legs and hands . . . he said now ye are made manifest; so the
> executioner being about to turn him off the ladder, he uttered this
> expression, saying, I suffer for Christ in whom I live, and for whom
> I die.[52]

Stephenson proceeds through a similar series of stages: The executioner performs a piece of pantomime, and the prisoner delivers another
portion of his speech. This narration of their execution makes it seem

more like a passion play than a penal proceeding. In this respect, Pearson follows a long tradition of imbuing such scenes with a theatrical nature that strains credulity. Foxe's Book of Martyrs owes some of its popularity to the appeal of these scenes; Ridley and Lattimer enjoy a similar parley on the day of their martyrdom, culminating when Lattimer tells Ridley that the advancing flames will "light such a candle, by God's Grace, in England, as I trust will never be put out."[53] Pearson echoes this ecstatic tone, concluding the body of his letter by commenting, "Thus the Faithful witnesses sealed their testimony for the Lord against the Dragons power, and blessedly departed with praises in their mouths, entering joyfully with their beloved into Everlasting Rest."[54]

These executions formed the staple of the second generation of Quaker sufferings. In one form or another, portions of material appearing in *A Call from Death to Life* found their way into a variety of martyrologies, including Bishop's *New England Judged*, and into Burrough's *A Declaration of the Sad and Great Persecution and Martyrdom of the People of God in New-England* (1660/1). Like a successful contemporary political campaign, these Quaker tracts managed to convey a coherent message through a variety of forms addressed to a variety of audiences.

IV: "I Will Stop that Vein"

Bishop's *New England Judged* was the omnibus of New England suffering, and it is this distillation of suffering that reached the hands of Charles I.[55] Compiling reprinted laws against Quakers, lists of fines, first-person accounts, and correspondence, Bishop detailed every offense against Quakers, from the executions in Boston, to two firkins of butter confiscated from Edward Perry in Plymouth.[56] Bishop does distinguish between major and minor persecutions, and treats the martyrdoms in more detail. His account of Robinson and Stephenson's deaths is consistent with the more immediate narrative in Peter Pearson's letter included in *A Call*, but considerably more detailed, suggesting that Bishop had either additional sources or a greater sense of drama.[57] Bishop includes the letter from Robinson to the court at Boston that appears in *A Call*.[58] Bishop also includes a letter from Stephenson, "a paper of his Call to the Work and Service of the Lord," that does not appear in *A Call*. This paper is a succinct and affecting narrative of his call from the plough in Yorkshire to the prison in Boston, by way of Barbados.[59] It is not clear why this paper does not appear in *A Call*, but it is a testament to the energetic and coordinated nature of Quaker publishing that this testimony of Stephenson's does reach readers in England. In a similar vein, Bishop includes a lengthy polemic signed by Stephenson and Robinson in the appendix to *New England Judged*.[60]

Bishop's work sets the stage for appeals from more influential Quakers directly to the King. Burrough's *A Declaration* takes Charles II as its explicit audience, but it appears that the sovereign's sympathy for such appeals was a product of an exchange that Bishop reports in *New England Judged*. Early Quaker historian William Sewel describes Charles II's response to the arrogance of a Bay Colony magistrate:

> "[Charles II] having got a book written by George Bishop, containing a relation of the cruel persecution in New England, and reading a passage concerning major-general Denison, who, to put off those who complained of their wicked proceeding, said 'This year you will go and complain to the Parliament, the next year they will send to see how it is; and in the third year the government is changed.' He took much notice of this, and calling to the lords to hear it, said 'Lo, these are my good subjects of New England: but I will put a stop to them.'"[61]

Denison's speech identifies the vagaries of colonial print culture that gave the Bay Colony relatively free rein to enforce its repressive policies, but it is also an observation bound to infuriate a sovereign. It may well be that Denison never said any such thing, but Bishop can avail himself of the same vagaries of Atlantic print culture and colonial administration by putting words in the mouth of Quaker tormentors. Bishop opens the door for Burrough, both literally, in the form of his narrative, and figuratively, in the form of the audience Burrough secured with Charles II.

In contrast to the exhaustive nature of *New England Judged*, *A Declaration of the Sad and Great Martyrdom of the People of God called Quakers, in New-England . . .* is effectively an executive summary of Quaker sufferings. The title page of this work functions almost as a broadside, summarizing the sufferings detailed inside. This text announces that it is "partly an answer to a Petition and Address of the Gen Court at Boston in New-England," but it transcends that occasion to make a broader appeal to the king.

A Declaration condenses the narratives of noncapital suffering, but it does treat the martyrdoms in some detail. The narrative of Stephenson and Robinson's execution is a close paraphrase of the Pearson letter first appearing in *A Call*, but in this context, its import is different. Addressing Charles II, they identify Massachusetts' leaders as those

> Who begun in immodesty, went on in inhumanity and cruelty, and were not satisfied until they had the blood of three of the martyrs of Jesus. Revenge for all which we do not seek, but lay them before Thee, considering Thou hast been well acquainted with Sufferings, and so mayest better consider them that suffer, and mayest for the future restrain the Violence of these Rulers of New-England.[62]

Burrough continues, reminding Charles II that Massachusetts magistrates are "but the children of thy family, of which Thou art Chief Ruler; Who have in divers of their proceedings forfeited their Patent.[63]

To underscore this point, Burrough includes a version of Mary Dyer's two executions that draws on the same sources as Bishop's account. Essentially, Burrough reworks material intended for the spiritual edification of Quaker brethren and uses it to support his request that Charles II "restrain the Violence of these Rulers of New-England." This printed petition provided Burrough an opportunity to make his case in person. As Sewel reports it, Burrough informed the King that "there was a vein of innocent blood opened in his dominions." The King responded, "But I will stop that vein."[64]

On 9 September 1661, Charles II did just that, issuing a writ of mandamus that tied the hands of Massachusetts as far as capital punishment was concerned. He declared:

> Having been informed that several of His Majesty's subjects among you, called Quakers . . . have been executed, and others (as hath been represented to us) are in danger to undergo the like; we have thought it fit to signify our pleasure in that behalf for the future, and do hereby require, that if there be any of those people called Quakers amongst you, now already condemned to suffer death . . . you are to forebear to proceed any further therein, but that you forthwith send the said persons over into their own kingdom of England . . . to the end such course shall be taken with them here as shall be agreeable to our laws, and their demerits.[65]

For the welfare of Quakers in New England, it was a small victory. Anticipating the possibility of such restraint, Massachusetts passed the infamous Cart and Whip Act in the spring of 1661, whereby instead of hanging, Quakers would be marched at the cart's tail out of the precincts of the colony, receiving ten stripes at each township on the way. It is true enough that this act of the king served only as a temporary restraint of the fury of Massachusetts, but it is a significant moment nonetheless: It illustrates the king taking the word of sectaries against the word of a government chartered by his father.

The word of these sectaries reached Charles II through ships bearing these words from New England, and presses circulating them in London. Atlantic print culture allowed Quakers to turn individual events of persecution into a critical resource for Quakers in general. At the same time, these Quaker tracts demonstrate that crossing the Atlantic can render authorship a more fluid category than it is traditionally construed. To point out that an ocean makes things fluid may seem like a tautology, but reviewing the Quaker deployment of more diffuse connections between colonial events and metropolitan texts reveals the rewards of close attention to the nuances of transatlantic publication. By suffering and subscribing, Quakers transformed the travels and travails of individuals into a cornerstone of a distinctly Atlantic religion.

CONCLUSION

"A Lively Experiment"

Quaker sufferings in New England reached their zenith as the Restoration occurred in England, and shaped the nature of their appeals to metropolitan authority. At the same time, the Restoration was a moment of great uncertainty for the inhabitants of Rhode Island, for the autonomy and freedom they enjoyed had been granted by various bodies acting without Royal warrant. Inevitably, the settlement of the colonies dictated by the new Stuart government would serve as a judgment on the proceedings over the years since Charles I had been in control; as an entity with no royal warrant, Rhode Island had more to lose than other colonies.

Indeed, For English men and women living in America, one of the critical issues of the restoration was the impact this change in government at home would have on the forms of their various governments in the colonies. As a restored king, Charles II might very reasonably wish to repudiate the work of the interregnum governments, including grants and patents issued in the name of Parliament or Protector, rather than King. American colonial leaders justly worried that Charles II might well choose to reshuffle extensively the boundaries and governments of his American possession. With the awareness that their survival depended upon the good will of the restored Stuart king, most colonies hastened to proclaim the new monarch as sovereign, and to dismiss their dealings with Parliament and commonwealth as meaningless expediency.[1]

With this shift in power at home, the colonies abroad were subject to many shifts and changes in the ensuing years, and many threats to their geographic territory, political autonomy, and corporate existence. For Clarke and Rhode Island, the most immediate threat came from

Connecticut and its representative, John Winthrop, Jr., who was eager to claim the shore of Narragansett Bay as the eastern boundary of his colony. In his suits to the king, Clarke faced a dual challenge: to preserve his colony from the claims of Connecticut, which would swallow up almost all of its territory, and to preserve the latitude Rhode Islanders enjoyed in religious affairs, even as the Stuart monarchy worked to enforce conformity at home. Coddington's coup had threatened the survival of Rhode Island during the Interregnum, but with the Restoration, Charles II could conceivably undo the work of Williams, Gorton, and Clarke with the stroke of his pen. Given the (literal) latitude granted Massachusetts in support of its claim to much of northern New England based on an interpretation of its charter placing the bounds of the colony three miles north of the source, not mouth, of the Merrimack, it would not have been much for Massachusetts, Connecticut, or Plymouth to stretch its patent a bit and extinguish Rhode Island entirely. On their own merits, Clarke's claims would seem to face long odds—he faced a well-connected and better financed rival in the younger John Winthrop, and neither the territorial claim nor the religious diversity of the colony could be imagined to have much natural sympathy with the imaginations of Charles II and his advisers.

The nullification of the Coddington commission was a comparatively straightforward affair, in that much of the colony was united against Coddington's usurpation of the government they had established. However, in Clarke's work for Rhode Island, in the administration of a restored Stuart monarch, he faced more formidable and varied adversaries from outside the precincts of the little colony. The language Clarke uses in his appeals to the King is the language he developed in *Ill Newes*. His effort depends to a large degree on the ability to explain how things are in what was a hazy and remote corner of the world, and of Charles II's imagination.

One factor working in Clarke's favor was the recent and successful example of Quaker appeals against the persecution of Massachusetts. Just as *Ill Newes* served the Quakers as a model for narrating colonial religious persecution, the ensuing flood of Quaker narratives of persecution served to create a discursive climate in which Clarke could reanimate his grievances in the context of similar Quaker narratives.

Clarke's campaign, to a large degree, depends upon the authority he can claim for himself, and the legacy of *Ill Newes* for him, is to give his appeals the clothing of authority. What Clarke does have is the authority of his experience, and his identity as an author of these experiences. In producing *Ill Newes*, Clarke authorizes himself, both in the sense of imbuing

himself with authority, and in the sense of making himself into an author.[2]
His petitions to the King revive the narrative of the travails he and his
fellows suffered, which has been given new relevance by the sufferings of
the Quakers, and he uses this experience as the foundation of a claim for
a charter that would preserve them and their liberties from the predations
of their neighbors.

I: "For Cause of Conscience"

The principal thrust of John Clarke's appeal to the King comes in two
petitions he prepared in January 1661/2. Clarke's ambitions for the charter
were twofold: He sought to preserve the territorial integrity of the settlements comprising Rhode Island and Providence Plantations, and to preserve the religious latitude its citizens enjoyed. In both respects Clarke
succeeded, and the two efforts are inevitably related. The obstacles to a
guarantee of religious freedom are the reservations of Charles, and more
especially his adviser Clarendon, while the obstacles to territorial integrity
came in the rival claims of Connecticut's John Winthrop, Jr. The principal concern here is with religious issues; while Clarke also prevailed in the
territorial questions, this result emerged as the result of negotiations with
Winthrop and Clarendon. James's biography of Clarke offers a detailed
narrative of these territorial negotiations; for the purposes of this study,
it is sufficient to know that Clarendon stalled the enrollment of the Connecticut charter on the strength of Clarke's representations that the charter violated Rhode Island's.[3]

Clarke's opening appeal to Charles II recapitulates the founding narrative of his settlement that he offers at the start of *Ill Newes*:

> Your petitioners were necessitated long since for causes of con-
> science, with respect to the worship and service of God, to take
> up a resolution to quit their deare and native country, and all their
> near and precious relations and enjoyments therein, and to expose
> themselves and their families to all the hazards and inconvenienc-
> es, which they might meete with upon the vast and swelling ocean
> or in the barbarous and howling wilderness to which they might
> come.[4]

At the outset this is an essentially straightforward recapitulation of any
migration of any first-generation New Englander. Indeed, this feature is

important to Clarke, for he here insists on the same normative position he occupies in *Ill Newes*. Clarke comes very close to misrepresenting whom he represents: "being thus resolved, they were, by the greatly obliging clemency of your Royal father permitted to prosecute this resolution of theirs." Conceivably, this phrase could refer to the recipients of the Massachusetts Bay Company charter of 1629, which was signed by Charles I, and has little to do with Rhode Island, or to the Providence patent of 1644, which had nothing to do with Charles I and was issued under the authority of his Parliamentary opponents.

This bit of obfuscation does help Clarke reconstitute the harassed origins and contentious history of the colony as a natural unfolding of English history. In the same vein, Clarke represents the divisions that led his party, along with Williams's and Gorton's, to move to Rhode Island as an anticipated stage in the English settlement of North America: "after a long encounter, with many perils of sea and robbers, [we] were by the good hand of the Lord safely conducted unto . . . those parts of America." Once in America, as Clarke explains, "for the aforesaid causes of conscience, and for peace sake, they were also necessitated to travaill further among the barbarians in places untroad and with no small hazard, to seek out a place of habitation."[5]

The challenges Clarke and his fellows faced are refigured as coming from their environment, and not their fellows: "Sea and robbers" and "barbarians in places untroad" are a gesture toward the actual challenges they faced, which were inflicted more by ministers and magistrates than by robbers and barbarians. In his address to the King, Clarke is discreet in his description of the differences among the English colonists. Choosing again not to present a persecuted and marginalized figure, Clarke allows only that his party was necessitated, for causes of conscience, to "travaill" further. This gesture toward their actual situation should have been enough to remind Charles and his advisers of Clarke's earlier reports from New England, especially since Clarendon would likely have been familiar with Clarke's story through his association with the prominent Baptist William Kiffin, who in 1663 was arrested because of an accusation of involvement in an Anabaptist plot against the King; a letter from him to Clarendon sufficed to secure his release immediately.[6] In fact, despite the gulf between their religious sentiments, English Baptists had made overtures to Charles II even when he was in exile. As Clarendon describes it, "They sent an address to the King by one of their party . . . they made very extravagant propositions, and seemed to depend much on the death of Cromwell, and thereupon to compute their own power to serve the King."[7]

Clarke continues his petition, explaining that this habitation, hazardous as it is, is a place where "according to what was propounded in your petitioners first adventure they might with freedome of conscience worship the Lord their God, as they were persuaded."[8] This liberty of conscience in Rhode Island is thus figured as the inverse of suffering in Massachusetts, and emerges as a foundational ideal of Rhode Island. Through Clarke's experience and travails, he constructs this ideal polemically, out of the persecuting and intransigent nature of Rhode Island's neighbors.

In this and other respects, Clarke presents a narrative to the King and his advisers that is reflected back to him with royal authorization. The petition narrates Clarke's dealings with the Indians in much the same way he does in *Ill Newes*, and this language is repeated back to him in the charter. The remainder of this first petition is essentially a narration of English history through Rhode Island eyes since the settlement of the colony. Not surprisingly, this narrative is adroit in its smoothing over two decades of very contentious history on both sides of the Atlantic.

Throughout this petition, Clarke displays a gift for understatement that borders on the disingenuous. Just as his fellows were "necessitated to travail further for causes of conscience," there are "Commissioners impowered from both his [Charles I's] houses of Parliament for the generall management of foreigne Plantations," with no mention that this body was created to seize control of the colonies from the King. Indeed, the petition generally expresses a desire for a tacit understanding between Clarke's government and the King's that each will treat the other as if its course has been foreordained and uneventful. It does no good for Clarke, or for the King, to dwell on the contested and interrupted state of their political power; their separate travails are the background of these documents, and Clarke frames his petition as a way to avoid future contention.

Like many such documents, this petition mimics the syntax of a sentence, with many clauses of exposition leading to a single request. In this petition, the expository clauses offer Clarke's narration of the travails of Rhode Island, but at the point where he finally makes his desires known to Charles II, he invokes the King's own experience of suffering, and indirectly, the martyrdom of Charles II's father: "Wherefore, O, King, seeing it hath pleased the most holy Majesty on high, the King of Kings, to remember you in your low and exiled state . . . whereby, as it were without hands, you have been restored to, and clothed with more excellent majesty and more absolute soveraigne power than your ancestors have attained unto."[9] The request that is the predicate of this description of the King's return is nothing less than a request for an unprecedented degree of religious latitude: "humbly craveing we may find such grace in your sight, whereby under the wing of your Royall protection, we may not only be sheltered, but caused to flourish in our civill and religious concernment in these remote parts of the world." Specifically, the trials Clarke has narrated to the King embolden him to state, "So shall your servants take themselves greatly obliged while they are quietly permitted with freedom of conscience to worship the Lord their God, as they are persuaded to pray for the life of the King."[10] In a London where Clarendon was working rapidly to narrow the latitude offered in the Declaration of Breda, such a request verged on impertinence.

Indeed, Clarke's second petition makes the same request in stronger language. This letter recapitulates the premises of the first petition, with the added guarantee that "the state of the case is such as really hath been presented unto your Majesty." Clarke continues, asserting a connection between the petitioners' Englishness, their travails and sufferings, and their loyalty to the King: "Wherefore your petitioners humbly pray your Majestys favourable aspect towards them, who have still in their removes, and in the rest of their actings made it manifest, that they as the true natives of England, have firmly adhered in their allegience and loyalty to the soveraignty thereof."[11] It is a curious array of ideas that Clarke attempts to draw together here. His claim that Rhode Islanders' identity as "true natives of England" rests on "their removes and actings" seems specious unless one reflects that these removes and actings were prompted by the persecution Clarke has represented as an affront to the dignity of an English subject. This persecution has been enacted by the Bay Colony's extralegal usurpation of the prerogatives of English law, which makes the Massachusetts ministers and magistrates bad subjects. If anything, as Clarke's petition unfolds, he claims that the persecution Clarke and his fellows have suffered has made them better English subjects, and more fit to serve the King.

Consequently, Clarke asks for a guarantee that his fellows will be permitted to continue as English subjects with the same privileges as they have been accustomed to enjoy. The petitioners "have it much on their hearts (if they may be permitted) to hold forth a lively experiment, that a flourishing civill State may stand, yea, and best be maintained, and that among English spirits, with a full liberty in religious concernments."

Clarke explains that the King can guarantee that this happy state is preserved. "[Y]our Royall subjects . . . hopefully craveing wee may find such grace in your sight as to receive from your Majesty a more absolute, ample and free charter of civill incorporation." Clarke informs the King that "under the wing of your Royall protection . . . we may not onley be sheltered, but . . . may be caused to flourish in our civill and religious concernments in these remote parts of the world . . . while [we] are quietly permitted with freedome of conscience to worship the Lord their God."[12] These phrases are virtually identical to the language to which Charles II put his seal, and which guaranteed the religious freedoms of Rhode Islanders for almost two centuries.[13]

II: "Our Trusty and Welbeloved Subject"

After some further negotiations over territorial details, Clarke sailed home with a charter for Rhode Island and Providence Plantations in 1663. The 1663 Rhode Island charter served as the foundation of the colony and state's government until 1843, when the Dorr rebellion led to a new constitution providing a broader franchise. Because of changes in England, however, it would be hard to see the 1663 Rhode Island charter as the beginning of a new paradigm for the relations between North American colonies and the English metropolis. The success that Williams, Gorton, and Clarke enjoyed in narrating their colony into existence did not inspire a legion of dissidents elsewhere in the colonies to follow their example. After the Restoration, and more still after the Glorious Revolution, the presence of royal agents and later governors representing the Crown in America foreclosed the opportunity for the kind of print representations Williams, Gorton, and Clarke were able to produce for metropolitan audiences.

At the same time, it is tempting, but misleading, to make a case that these dissidents offered a template for the dissent that culminated in the Declaration of Independence in 1776. The efforts of New England dissidents in the seventeenth century did create a zone of relative freedom and autonomy in Rhode Island, but this liberty was a concession granted to the colony by the sovereign, in the context of an ongoing colonial relation.

As an artifact of this relation, this royal document functions as a mirror for *Ill Newes* and Clarke's petitions, reflecting his narrative back across the Atlantic, imbued with royal authority. To establish the warrant for the charter, the preamble offers a précis of the origins of the settlements that made up Rhode Island. This account of settlement, however, is a highly particular one: It removes any sense of opposition to the suit of the grantees from its narrative. This account begins by describing the impulse to found the colony. The charter explains that

> Whereas, we have been informed, by the petition of our trusty and well-beloved subject, John Clarke [et al.] . . . that they, pursuing, with peaceable and loyal minds, their sober, serious, and religious intentions, of godly edifying themselves, and one another, in the holy Christian faith and worship, as they were persuaded . . . did, not only by the consent and good encouragement of our royal progenitors, transport themselves out of this kingdom of England into America.[14]

In essence, this recapitulates the description in Clarke's petition of his party's "resolution to quit their deare and native country." In some respects, this language is akin to similar colonial documents, but the authorities in Massachusetts who expelled Rhode Island founders Roger Williams and Samuel Gorton, and imprisoned John Clarke, would be unlikely to describe the emigrations of these men as the result of "sober, serious, and religious intentions." Moreover, the edifying these men came to do has no other foundation than "faith and worship, as they were persuaded."

While this language could be contested by opponents of Rhode Island, including John Winthrop, Jr., the charter endorses Clarke's narrative. The preamble also implies that individual conscience is the basis of religious belief, foreshadowing the rights guaranteed in the charter. The preamble continues, delicately narrating the adventures of these dissident settlers in an almost euphemistic tone:

> after their first settlement amongst other our subjects in those parts, for the avoiding of discord, and those many evils which were likely to ensure upon some of those subjects not being able to bear, in these remote parts, their different apprehensions in religious concernments, and in pursuance of the aforesaid ends, did once again leave their desirable stations and habitations.[15]

What the charter describes here as "avoiding of discord," by the Rhode Island settlers, because of "their different apprehensions in religious concernments," many in Massachusetts would call the expulsion of heretical and seditious radicals. In its delicate elision of these controversies, the charter again echoes Clarke's petition. As we have seen, in addition to Clarke's troubles, Roger Williams was banished from his "desirable station" in Salem for insistently advocating total separation from the Church of England, while Samuel Gorton was forced to leave numerous "desirable habitations" throughout southeastern New England because of his religious radicalism and general contempt for authority. Anne Hutchinson and her Antinomian followers settled the towns of Portsmouth and Newport after leaving Massachusetts voluntarily or under duress. To characterize the actions of the Massachusetts court against Antinomians, Gortonoges, Baptists, and Quakers simply as "not being able to bear, in these remote parts, their different apprehensions in religious concernments" is disingenuous understatement.[16] Nonetheless, it is a circumlocution that grants equal credence to the "concernments" of all parties; as in Clarke's description, it is as if the various parties agree to disagree, and go their separate ways. The trouble Clarke describes in *Ill Newes* is present, but not articulated.

The preamble further asserts that the Rhode Island settlers "with excessive labor and travel, hazard and charge did transplant themselves into the midst of the Indian natives, who as we are informed, are the most potent princes and people of all that country." As a result of this proximity, the Rhode Island settlers "are seized and possessed, by purchase and consent of the said natives, to their full content, of such lands, islands, rivers, harbors and roads, as are very convenient, both for plantations, and also for building of ships."[17] The charter's description of the economic potential of the Narragansett region is indisputable; it was this wealth that inspired numerous claims on the region by Massachusetts, Plymouth, and Connecticut. Many of these competing claims were justified by claiming that the Rhode Island settlers had not, in fact, bargained with the "most potent princes and people of that country," but rather with upstart petty chiefs with no right to sell land. Against this claim, however, the dissident version of events is specifically narrated in the charter; the language of the charter supports the sovereignty and legal standing in land transactions of these potent princes and people that is central in Williams's and Gorton's narratives. More specifically, this account echoes Clarke's reckoning of the resources of the place, and his narrative of the acquisition of the land in his introduction to *Ill Newes*.

In a similar vein, the charter is silent on the unusual source of title to these lands: Unlike neighboring colonists, Rhode Island's settlers did not come there with a patent, charter, or grant from London already in hand. Instead, settlers around the Narragansett Bay purchased land from local Indians. However, purchasing land piecemeal from indigenous inhabitants undermined the grandiose conception of the power of the English sovereign exhibited in gestures like the 1620 grant to the Council for New England of all of North America from sea to sea that lay between 40 and 48 degrees of latitude. To say the least, the idea that a right to New World lands came from negotiations with Native Americans, rather than with a warrant from the Crown, contradicted the prevailing colonial doctrine of the time.

Thus having literally and figuratively established the grounds of the petition to the King, the charter explains that "whereas, in their humble address, they have freely declared, that it is much on their hearts (if they may be permitted) to hold forth a lively experiment, that a most flourishing civil state may stand and best be maintained, and that among our English subjects, with a full liberty in religious concernments."[18] This "lively experiment," the charter continues, will be as good for the King as for his subjects: This experiment also postulates "that true piety rightly grounded upon gospel principles, will give the best and greatest security to sovereignty, and will lay in the hearts of men the strongest obligations to true loyalty."[19] This passage actually adopts, verbatim, the language of Clarke's second petition. Moreover, Clarke's phrase, "lively experiment," comes directly from *Ill Newes*. "Lively experiment" has been a popular way for historians to describe the frame of government that made Rhode Island unique among American colonies. The phrase originally occurs in Clarke's discussion of his assertion that Christ is "the Anointed Prophet, none to him in point of instruction." As he explains, "he it is in whose hand is the Key of David, and he openeth the heart to understand the scriptures; to shew a lively experiment of his powerfull instructing, when he was here upon earth, he . . . called the illiterate and foolish Fishermen . . . that as a teacher he might shew his abilities."[20]

As this context makes clear, "experiment" had a different use in the middle of the seventeenth century than it does today. Clarke uses it to suggest a demonstration that is taking place, rather than a trial that will reveal some piece of information in the future when it is finished. The Oxford English Dictionary confirms this sense, with one sense of the word from Clarke's time being "Practical acquaintance with a person or thing; experience; an instance of this"—also, "practical proof, a specimen, and example."[21] The "experiment" in Rhode Island is not a trial of a hypothetical question, but an ongoing demonstration of the benefit of framing a government that does not dictate religious practice.

The charter supports this "experiment": "Now, know ye, that we, being willing to Encourage the hopeful undertaking of our said loyal and loving subjects, and to secure them in the free exercise and enjoyment of all their civil and religious rights, appertaining to them, as our loving subjects."[22] Even as it insists upon the English subjectivity of these colonial petitioners, the charter explicitly identifies Charles II's church as the institution from which freedom is needed: "because some of the people and inhabitants of the same colony cannot, in their private opinions, conform to the public exercise of religion, according to the liturgy, forms and ceremonies of the Church of England."[23] The charter thus guarantees "That our royal will and pleasure is, that no person within the said colony, at any time hereafter shall be any wise molested, punished, disquieted, or called in question, for any differences in opinion in matters of religion."[24]

The charter specifies this right not only in terms of checks on the state, but also in terms of the freedom of the individual: "all and every person and persons may, from time to time, and at all times hereafter, freely and fully have and enjoy his and their own judgments and consciences, in matters of religious concernments, throughout the tract of land hereafter mentioned."[25] Even with the proviso "they behaving themselves peaceable and quietly, and not using this liberty to licentiousness and profaneness, nor to the civil injury or outward disturbance of others, any law, statute, or clause therein contained," John Clarke secured a remarkable degree of religious liberty for Rhode Island. As a result of his decade in London, the ideology of the suffering English subject he brought with him from America becomes a law guaranteeing the freedom of English subjects from such suffering.

The language Clarke uses to narrate his persecution at the hands of Massachusetts becomes the language that guarantees Rhode Island's freedom from this persecution. For Clarke, the language of his dissent is literally authorized with the seal of the King. In one sense, Clarke's salient accomplishment is the instantiation of religious suffering as a form of witness almost the equivalent of martyrdom. For the dissident, a recognizable persecution that does not kill him or her has obvious attractions. What Clarke develops is a witness with the bloody attractions of martyrdom, but one that he survives. Obviously, the stories of Clarke, Holmes, and Crandall do not match Foxe's narratives of Ridley, Cranmer, and Lattimer, but the suffering of the New England Baptists distinguishes the abstractions of Williams's *Bloody Tenent yet more Bloody* from the narrative of *Ill Newes* as an effective work of dissent. It was this persecution at the hands of the Massachusetts magistrates that was the genesis of the document that protected not just Clarke and his Anabaptist fellows, but their Antinomian neighbors on Aquidneck, Williams and his Providence neighbors, Gorton's party in Warwick, and even Quakers, whose presence in Rhode Island would expand dramatically over the next decades. The 1663 Rhode Island charter shows experiences of colonial persecution transformed into metropolitan dissenting narratives, returned to America in the language of colonial power.

NOTES

INTRODUCTION

(pp. 1–15)

1. "Charter of Rhode Island and Providence Plantations," in *The Federal and State Constitutions Colonial Charters, and Other Organic Laws of the States, Territories, and Colonies Now or Heretofore Forming the United States of America*, ed. Francis Newton Thorpe (Washington, D.C.: Government Printing Office, 1909). Via http://www.yale.edu/lawweb/avalon/states/ri04.htm#1 accessed 3 February 2007. Hereafter abbreviated as "Charter."

2. The term "Rhode Island" can be confusing, as it is both the familiar name for the colony formally designated "Rhode Island and Providence Plantations" and the name for the island containing the settlements of Portsmouth and Newport, known as "The Island of Rhode Island." To avoid confusion between these distinct but overlapping entities, I will use "Aquidneck," the original name of the island, to refer specifically to the island, and "Rhode Island" to refer to the colony at large.

3. I use the term "dissident" rather than "dissenter" because "dissident" has a broader connotation embracing political dissent, and to avoid confusion with Dissenters, a term applied to Protestants who separated themselves from the communion of the Church of England in the later seventeenth century.

4. Quakers did not come to America until after the Rhode Island towns were settled, but many of the colony's founders eventually embraced the faith; by the late 1650s, the colony had become a popular entrepot for Quakers traveling to more orthodox colonies. See Carla Pestana, *Quakers and Baptists in Colonial Massachusetts* (Cambridge: Cambridge University Press, 1991); Rufus Jones, *The Quakers in the American Colonies* (New York: Norton, 1966), pp. 52–3. Examples of heresiographies include the various parts and editions of Thomas Edwards's

Gangraena, and Ephraim Pagitt's *Heresiography*, which went through several editions from 1645 to 1662.

5. David Zaret, *The Origins of Democratic Culture: Printing, Petitions, and the Public Sphere in Early-Modern England* (Princeton, N.J.: Princeton University Press, 2000), p. 99.

6. Homi Bhabha, "Sly Civility," in *The Location of Culture* (London: Routledge, 1994), p. 93.

7. Myra Jehlen, "The Literature of Colonization," in Sacvan Bercovitch, ed., *The Cambridge History of American Literature*, Vol. I. (Cambridge: Cambridge University Press, 1994), p. 36.

8. The Bay Colony was more successful in similar efforts it made to expand on its northern border. See Jeremy Belknap, *The History of New Hampshire* (New York: Johnson Reprint Co., 1970), I: 17–34.

9. For more on Anne Hutchinson and print culture, see Jonathan Beecher Field, "The Antinomian Controversy Did Not Take Place," *Early American Studies* Fall 2008, 448–463.

10. Philip Gura, *A Glimpse of Sion's Glory: Puritan Radicalism in New England 1620–1660* (Middletown, Conn.: Wesleyan University Press, 1984), p. 5.

11. Stephen Foster, *The Long Argument: English Puritanism and the Shaping of New England Culture, 1500-1700* (Chapel Hill: UNC Press/Institute for Early American History and Culture, 1991), p. 190.

12. Stephen Foster, "New England and the Challenge of Heresy, 1630 to 1660: The Puritan Crisis in Transatlantic Perspective," *The William and Mary Quarterly*, 3rd Ser., Vol. 38, No. 4. (Oct. 1981), pp. 658–9.

13. Andrew R. Murphy, *Conscience and Community: Revisiting Toleration and Religious Dissent in Early Modern England and America* (University Park: Pennsylvania State University Press, 2001), p. 27.

14. Darren Staloff, *The Making of an American Thinking Class: Intellectuals and Intelligentsia in Puritan Massachusetts* (New York: Oxford University Press, 1998).

15. Stephen Foster, *The Long Argument*; Janice Knight, *Orthodoxies in Massachusetts: Rereading American Puritanism* (Cambridge, Mass.: Harvard University Press, 1994).

16. Louise Breen, *Transgressing the Bounds: Subversive Enterprises among the Puritan Elite in Massachusetts, 1630–1692* (Oxford: Oxford University Press, 2001); Lisa Gordis, *Opening Scripture: Bible Reading and Interpretive Authority in Puritan New England* (Chicago: University of Chicago Press, 2002).

17. As early as 1652, John Clarke was force to distinguish between the geographic sense of New England, and the intellectual sense of New England. See John Clarke, *Ill Newes from New-England, or, A nar[r]ative of New-Englands persecution: wherin is declared that while old England is becoming new, New-England is become old : also four proposals to the Honoured Parliament and Councel of State, touching the way to propagate the Gospel of Christ . . . : also four conclusions touching the faith and*

order of the Gospel of Christ out of his last will and testament, confirmed and justified (London: Henry Hills, 1652), p. xvi.

18. Samuel Gorton, *An Incorruptible Key Composed of the Cx Psalme . . .* ([London]: 1647), p. [x].

19. Trish Loughran, *The Republic in Print: Print Culture in the Age of U.S. Nation Building* (New York: Columbia University Press, 2007), p. 6.

20. Loughran, p. 80.

21. Loughran, pp. 167, 252.

22. As an example of this perspective, a one-page summary of earlier "controversies" in *Entertaining Satan* speaks of passing "religious challenges from Baptists and followers of the Rhode Island sectarian Samuel Gorton," and "confrontation" with Quakers in "1660–61." John Demos, *Entertaining Satan: Witchcraft and the Culture of Early New England* (Oxford: Oxford University Press, 1982), pp. 379–80.

23. Governor Edmund Andros' efforts to use the Third Church of Boston for Anglican services are a notable example of this sort of interference, albeit one forestalled by the upheavals of the Glorious Revolution. See Perry Miller, *The New England Mind: From Colony to Province* (Cambridge, Mass.: Belknap Press of Harvard University Press, 1953), pp. 149–50.

24. For example, the parliamentarians who formed the core of the Committee for Foreign Plantations in 1643 were also the heart of the Parliamentary opposition to Charles II in the early 1640s. See Christopher Hill, *The Intellectual Origins of the English Revolution Revisited* (Oxford: Clarendon Press, 1997), p. 90.

25. Elizabeth Maddock Dillon, *The Gender of Freedom: Fictions of Liberalism and the Literary Public Sphere* (Stanford, Calif.: Stanford University Press, 2004), p. 77.

26. Dillon, p. 77.

27. Grantland Rice, *The Transformation of Authorship in Early America* (Chicago: University of Chicago Press, 1997), p. 24.

1. 50% COTTON:
Authorship, Authority, and the Atlantic
(pp. 17–24)

1. The sequence of Williams's publications during this first trip to London: *A Key into the Language of America*, 7 September 1643; *Mister Cotton's Letter Examined*, 5 February 1643/4; *Queries of Highest Consideration*, 9 February 1643/4; *The Bloudy Tenent of Persecution*, 15 July 1644; *Christenings Make Not Christians*, early 1645.

2. For example, Alan Heimert and Andrew Delbanco, eds., *The Puritans in America: A Narrative Anthology* (Cambridge, Mass.: Harvard University Press, 1985), p. 196, anthologize excerpts from *The Bloudy Tenent*, Cotton's *The Bloudy*

Tenent Washed, and Williams's *Experiments of Spiritual Life* under the rubric of the "Cotton–Williams Debate."

3. Murphy, pp. 48–54.

4. Zaret, pp. 176–84, 174.

5. Zaret, *Origins*, p. 177.

6. Perry Miller, "Errand into the Wilderness," in *Errand into the Wilderness* (Cambridge, Mass.: Belknap Press of Harvard University Press, 1984), p. 3. To judge from the usage history for "errand" in the Oxford English Dictionary, the distinction between these two senses is not quite as stark as Miller suggests.

7. See David D. Hall, "Introduction," in *The Colonial Book in the Atlantic World*, ed. Hugh Amory and David D. Hall (Cambridge: Cambridge University Press, 2000), p. 7.

8. These quantitative measures are imprecise. *Early English Books Online* includes North American imprints, and *European Americana* includes items in languages besides English. At the same time, a number of the Massachusetts imprints are essentially pro forma items related to Harvard commencements. In any event, the relative levels of publishing activity in London and Boston indicate the ongoing centrality of London presses for American authors in this period.

9. Philip Round, *By Nature and Custom Cursed: Transatlantic Civil Discourse and New England Cultural Production, 1620–1660* (Hanover, N.H.: Tufts/University Press of New England, 1999), p. 27.

10. Evans, digital edition, indicates that *Spiritual Milk for Boston babes in either England. Drawn out of the Breasts of both Testaments for their souls nourishment, but may be of like use to any children* (Boston: 1656) is the first individual American imprint for Cotton; he is credited as one of the authors of both the *Bay Psalm Book* (1640) and the *Cambridge Platform* (1649), which were collective efforts of the Bay Colony clerical elite.

11. The publisher of this letter was Benjamin Allen, who was an active publisher of materials relating to New England and a supporter of the Parliamentary cause. (See his entry in Henry R. Plomer, *A Dictionary of the Booksellers and Printers who Were at Work in England, Scotland and Ireland from 1641 to 1667* (London: for the Bibliographical Society, by Blades, East & Blades), 1907). Allen's motivations may have been either mercenary or ideological. While Cotton's writings were evidently quite popular, and could be expected to sell well, this letter obviously does not show him in a flattering light. Allen's widow, Hannah, published Cotton's last word in this debate, *The Bloudy Tenent, Washed and Made White . . .*, and married Livewell Chapman, a noted radical printer of the 1650s. See Leona Rostenberg, *Literary, Political, Scientific, Religious & Legal Publishing, Printing & Bookselling in England, 1551–1700* (New York: B. Franklin, 1965).

12. For the publication date of Cotton's letter, see Hugh Spurgin, *Roger Williams and Puritan Radicalism in the English Separatist Tradition*, Studies in American Religion V. 34 (Lewiston, Me.: Edwin Menwell, 1989), p. 37.

13. See Larzer Ziuff, *The Career of John Cotton: Puritanism and the American Experience* (Princeton, N.J.: Princeton University Press, 1962), pp. 261–71, for estimates of the gaps between the composition and publication of Cotton's work.

14. John Cotton, *A Reply to Mr. Williams his Examination, Publications of the Narragansett Club* (Providence: 1867), II: 9.

15. Cotton, *A Reply*, pp. 9–10.

16. Glenn LaFantasie, ed., *The Correspondence of Roger Williams* (Hanover, N.H., and London: Brown University Press/University Press of New England, 1988), I: 32.

17. John Cotton, *The Way of Life* (London: By M.F. for Luke Fawne, and S. Gelibrand, 1641) p. [A 5–6].

18. Cotton, *The Powring out of the Seven Vials* (London: for R. S. and to be sold at Henry Overton's shop, 1641), p. A2.

19. Quoted in Chester N. Greenough, "On Authorship of Singing Psalms a Gospel Ordinance," *Transactions of the Colonial Society of Massachusetts*, Vol. XX (1917–1919), p. 246.

20. See David Zaret, "Religion, Science and Printing in the Public Spheres in Seventeenth-Century England," in *Habermas and the Public Sphere*, ed. Craig C. Calhoun (Cambridge, Mass.: MIT Press, 1992), p. 213.

21. Everett Emerson, *John Cotton* (Rev. ed.) (Boston: Twayne, 1990), pp. 20–1.

22. Round, p. 28.

23. Round, pp. 144, 170; Gura, p. 172; Hall, p. 367; Tuttle, p. 372.

2. A KEY FOR THE GATE:
Roger Williams, Parliament, & Providence
(pp. 26–47)

1. Edwin Gaustad, *Liberty of Conscience: Roger Williams in America* (Grand Rapids, Mich.: William B. Eerdmans, 1991), p. xi.

2. James Axtell, *The European and the Indian* (New York: Oxford University Press, 1981), pp. 135, 203.

3. Perry Miller, "Errand into the Wilderness," in *Errand into the Wilderness* (Cambridge, Mass.: Harvard University Press, 1956), p. 15.

4. For specific dates in this section, I am indebted to Glenn LaFantasie's "Roger Williams Chronology" in Glenn LaFantasie, ed., *The Correspondence of Roger Williams*, I: xcii. Dates are given without conversion from the Julian, or Old Style calendar, to the Gregorian, or new Style calendar. Under the Julian calendar, the new year began on 25 March, but dates between 1 January and 24 March were rendered using both years, as in 30 January 1648/9. Date usage in this text follows this practice.

5. See, for example, the charter of the Massachusetts Bay Company. Nathaniel

B. Shurtleff, ed., *The Records of the Governor and Company of the Massachusetts Bay* (Boston: 1853), I: 3. Here, as in other cases, Williams's unconventional position on Indian affairs was dictated more by the mandates of his faith than by a sense of fair play for the Indians. Williams objected to this grant not simply because it denigrated the humanity and sovereignty of Indians, but because it depended on the notion of "Christendom," and for Williams, "the terms Christian and Christendom could not properly be applied to a *nation*, since only the *church* actually consisted of God's chosen people." W. Clark Gilpin, *The Millenarian Piety of Roger Williams* (Chicago: University of Chicago Press, 1979), p. 41.

6. John Russell Bartlett, ed., *Records of the Colony of Rhode Island and Providence Plantations* (Providence, R.I.: NP, 1856), I: 18. Hereafter cited as RCRI.

7. RCRI, I: 27–31.

8. Howard M. Chapin, *A Documentary History of Rhode Island* (Providence, R.I.: Preston and Rounds, 1916), I: 217; John Winthrop, *The Journal of John Winthrop, 1630–1649*, ed. Richard S. Dunn, James Savage, and Laetitia Yandle (Cambridge, Mass.: Belknap Press of Harvard University Press, 1996), pp. 540–1. The date of Williams's departure is necessarily an approximation, as the vagaries of weather and shipping could cause the time a passage took to vary widely. Cressy suggests "eight to twelve weeks or more"; at that rate, even with a very speedy passage, Williams could not have hung around London for long after the appearance of the *Bloudy Tenent*, and he may well have been gone before it appeared. David Cressy, *Coming Over: Migration and Communication between England and New England in the Seventeenth Century* (Cambridge: Cambridge University Press, 1987), p. 151.

9. Roger Williams, *Queries of Highest Consideration*. Publications of the Narragansett Club (Providence: NP, 1866), II: 256.

10. William Wood, *New Englands Prospect* (London: 1634), t.p.

11. Glenn LaFantasie, "Lost Correspondence and Incomplete Records." Editorial note, CRW, I: 216.

12. Laura J. Murray, "Vocabularies of Native American Languages: A Literary and Historical Approach to an Elusive Genre," *American Quarterly*, Vol. 53, No. 4 (December, 2001), pp. 594–5; see also Stephen A. Guice, "Early New England Missionary Linguistics," in *Papers in the History of Linguistics: Proceedings of the Third International Conference on the History of the Language Sciences . . . 1984* (Philadelphia: John Benjamins, 1987).

13. Adrian Johns, *The Nature of the Book: Print and Knowledge in the Making* (Chicago: University of Chicago Press, 1998), pp. 224–5.

14. Robert Fitzgibbon Young, *Comenius in England* (London: Oxford University Press/Harvey Milford, 1932), pp. 27, 61.

15. Barbara K. Lewalski, "Milton and the Hartlib Circle: Educational Projects and Epic Paideia," in *Literary Milton: Text, Pretext, Context*, ed. Diana Trevi-

ño Benet and Michael Leib (Pittsburgh: Duquesne University Press, 1994), p. 206–7.

16. As quoted in David Masson, *The Life of John Milton, Narrated in Connexion with the Political, Ecclesiastical, and Literary History of his Time* (London: MacMillan & Co., 1873), III: 200; for an exposition of the larger Comenian educational project, see Charles Webster, *The Great Instauration: Science, Medicine, and Reform, 1626–1600* (New York: Holmes and Meier, 1975), pp. 100–29.

17. Young, p. 61. That a form developed by a Jesuit missionary to teach Indians Latin could be deployed by Protestants for vulgar tongues suggests the dangerous versatility of this genre.

18. Anne G. Myles, "Dissent and the Frontier of Translation: Roger Williams's A Key into the Language of America," in *Possible Pasts: Becoming Colonial in Early America*, ed. Robert Blair St. George (Ithaca, N.Y.: Cornell University Press, 2000), p. 96.

19. Christopher Hill, *The Intellectual Origins of the English Revolution Revisited* (Oxford: Clarendon Press, 1997), p. 90. Hill writes: "When in the sixteen-thirties Hartlib, Drury and Comenius tried to give effect to Bacon's plans, their most enthusiastic supporter was John Pym; backed by the Earls of Bedford, Essex, Leicester, Pembroke, Salisbury and Warwick, by Lord Brooke, Lord Mandeville, Lord Wharton, Sir Thomas Roe, Sir Benjamin Rudyerd, Sir Thomas Barrington, Sir Nathaniel Rich, Sir William Waller, Sir Arthur Annesley, Sir John Clotworthy, John Selden, Oliver St. John." For the membership of the Providence Island Company, see Karen Ordahl Kupperman, *Providence Island, 1630–1641: The Other Puritan Colony* (Cambridge: Cambridge University Press, 1993).

20. Robert Brenner, *Merchants and Revolution: Commercial Change, Political Conflict, and London's Overseas Traders, 1550–1653* (London: Verso, 2003), p. 243.

21. Young, pp. 39, 52. At the end of this decade, Gauden's career took another turn: He appears to have aided in the composition of Charles I's *Eikon Basilike*. See Francis Falconer Madan, *New Bibliography of the Eikon Basilike* (London: B. Quaritch, 1950).

22. Robert Fitzgibbon Young, "Comenius and the Indians of New England" (London: King's College, 1929), p. 9. In *Comenius in England*, Young explains, "The implicit association of the plan for a college for scientific research with a general reform of schools and with the educational work that was being carried on among the colonists and the Indians in New England and Virginia is particularly significant, and is peculiar to Comenius and his follower, G.W. Leibniz. It must be remembered that one of the principal functions of scientific societies at this period was to digest and explain the vast body of fresh data on various bodies of knowledge which had been obtained from the Americas" (p. 7).

23. Young, *Comenius in England*, p. 61.

24. *New Englands First Fruits* (London: 1643), p. A2.

25. See Cotton Mather, *Magnalia Christii American* (Hartford: Silas Andrus, 1853), II: 14.

26. Will S. Monroe, *Comenius and the Beginnings of Educational Reform* (New York: 1900), pp. 78–81; for the persistence of this story, see especially J. B. Conant, "Comenius and Harvard," in *The Teacher of Nations* (Cambridge: The University Press, 1942), p. 40.

27. One of the premises underlying the English appropriation of American lands was a notion that Native Americans could hold no title to land because they did not settle and inhabit it in ways that were recognizable to English observers. See William Cronon, *Changes in the Land: Indians, Colonists, and the Ecology of New England* (New York: Hill and Wang, 1983), chaps. 2–3.

28. Myra Jehlen, "Three Writers of Early America," in *The Cambridge History of American Literature*, ed. Sacvan Bercovitch (Cambridge: Cambridge University Press, 1994), p. 77.

29. Ivy Schweitzer, *The Work of Self-Representation: Lyric Poetry in Colonial New England* (Chapel Hill: University of North Carolina Press, 1991), pp. 181–228.

30. See Roger Williams, *A Key into the Language of America*, ed. with a critical introduction, notes, and commentary by John J. Teunessen and Evelyn J. Hinz (Detroit: Wayne State University Press, 1973), pp. 14–23. For a survey of the structure and function of emblem books in this era, see Peter M. Daly, Literature in Light of the Emblem: Structural Parallels Between the Emblem and Literature in the Sixteenth and Seventeenth Centuries, 2nd ed., (Toronto: University of Toronto Press, 1998).

31. Roger Williams, *A Key into the Language of America . . . .* (London: Gregory Dexter, 1643, rpt. 1997), preface. Hereafter abbreviated *Key*.

32. Jehlen, p. 79.

33. Mary Louise Pratt, *Imperial Eyes: Travel Writing and Transculturation* (London: Routledge, 1992), p. 6.

34. *Key*, p.2.

35. Murray, p. 594; see Karen Ordahl Kupperman, *Indians and English: Facing off in Early America* (Ithaca, N.Y.: Cornell University Press, 2000), p. 81.

36. *Key*, n.p.

37. Gordon Sayre, *Les Sauvages Americains: Representations of Native Americans in French and English Colonial Literature* (Chapel Hill: University of North Carolina Press, 1997), p. 198.

38. *Key*, pp. 9–10.

39. *New Englands First Fruits* (London: R.O. & G[regory] D[exter] for Henry Overton, 1643, p. A2. Reprinted in Samuel Eliot Morrison, *The Founding of Harvard College* (Cambridge, Mass.: Harvard University Press, 1995), pp. 420–47. This comment is one of many examples that one might furnish of the automatic, near unconscious equation of Christianity and civilization. This same equation that the Bay Colony's boosters make in the 1640s, generations of historians

continued to make: Young comments of the Comenians that "one of the functions of the great scientific society would be to promote the extension of the Christian civilization of western Europe among the Indians of North America and the Moslems of the Near East." More recently, Alden Vaughn describes early missionary efforts thusly: "James, sagamore of the Lynn and Marblehead region, appeared willing to be civilized and converted." *New England Frontier,* 3rd ed. (Norman: University of Oklahoma Press, 1995), p. 241. Today, one imagines, most scholars of Native Americans would not make this kind of mistake, but the persistent conflation of Christianity and civilization in the historiography of early America can obscure the possibility of their separation.

40. *Key,* p. 54.

41. *Key,* p. 53.

42. *Key,* p. 64.

43. Thomas Morton, *New English Canaan* (London: 1631), p. 135; *Key,* p. 29.

44. *Key,* p. 95.

45. *Key,* p. 10.

46. *Key,* p. 85.

47. *Key,* p. 204.

48. Chapin, I: 212.

49. Chapin, I: 212.

50. Chapin, I: 212.

51. Chapin, I: 212–13.

52. Chapin, I: 215.

53. Shurtleff, I: 3.

54. Chapin, I: 216.

55. Shurtleff, I: 17.

56. Chapin, I: 215–16.

57. Chapin, I: 216

58. Chapin, I: 216.

59. RCRI, I: 28.

60. The Committee for Foreign Plantations was composed of the following men. Names appearing on the Williams charter are underlined, and those on the invalid Weld–Peter charter are italicized: Lords: *Robert, Earl of Warwick, Governor-in Chief,* Philip Earl of Pembroke, *Edward, Earl of Manchester,* William, Viscount Saye and Seale, Philip, Lord Wharton *John, Lord Roberts.*

Peers: Sir Gilbert Gerard, Baronet, *Sir Arthur Hasselrige, Baronet,* Sir Henry Vane, Jr. Knight, *Sir Benjamin Rudyer, Knight.*

Commons: (John Pym, Dec'd) Oliver Cromwell, *Dennis Bond, Miles Corbet,* Cornelius Holland, *Samuel Vassal,* John Rolle, *William Spurstow.* Some members appear to have signed both, but since many aspects of the validity of the Weld–Peter charter are in question, the signatures are difficult to verify; see Raymond Stearns, "The Weld–Peter Mission to England," *Publications of the Colonial Society of Massachusetts,* Vol. XXXII (1937), pp. 221–3, 233–6. In his biography of Williams, Samuel Brockunier observes: "The influence of Vane, Wharton, and Saye was probably decisive in winning over Sir Arthur Hasselrige, and the Earl of Warwick, who had previously signed the Weld patent." Samuel Brockunier, *The Irrepressible Democrat, Roger Williams* (New York: Ronald Press, 1940), p. 88.

3. "A BELCHER-OUT OF ERROURS": *Samuel Gorton and the Atlantic Subject* (pp. 48–70)

1. Nathaniel Morton, *New Englands Memorial* (Cambridge: 1669), pp. 108–10.

2. Samuel Gorton, "Samuel Gorton's Letter to Nathaniel Morton," in *Tracts and Other Papers Relating Principally to the Origin, Settlement, and Progress of the Colonies in North America,* ed. Peter Force (New York: Peter Smith, 1947), Vol. IV, number 7, p. 14.

3. Philip Gura, *A Glimpse of Sion's Glory: Puritan Radicalism in New England 1620–1660* (Middletown, Conn.: Wesleyan University Press, 1984), p. 303.

4. Christopher Hill, *The World Turned Upside Down: Radical Ideas During the English Revolution* (London: Penguin, 1991); Nigel Smith, *Perfection Proclaimed: Language and Literature in the English Radical Religion, 1640–1660* (Oxford: Oxford University Press, 1989).

5. Gura, p. 278.

6. *Correspondence of Roger Williams,* I: 215.

7. For details of this trial, see Jonathan Beecher Field, "The Grounds of Dissent: Heresies and Colonies in Colonial New England," Ph.D. Diss., University of Chicago, 2004, pp. 93–5.

8. *Simplicities Defence,* p. 44. Hereafter cited as SD.

9. Hall, p. 218.

10. Myles, p. 82.

11. Hall, p. 219.

12. See chapter 1.

13. SD, pp. 150–1.

14. SD, p. 151.

15. SD, p. 152.

16. John Winthrop, *The Journal of John Winthrop, 1630–1649,* ed. Richard S. Dunn, James Savage, and Laetitia Yandle (Cambridge, Mass.: Belknap Press of Harvard University Press, 1996), p. 413. Hereafter cited as JWJ.

17. SD, p. 153.

18. SD, p. 153.

19. SD, p. 153.

20. Stephen Greenblatt, *Renaissance Self-Fashioning: From More to Shakespeare* (Chicago: University of Chicago Press, 1980), pp. 226–7.

21. SD, p. 153.

22. SD, p. 153.

23. Stephen Greenblatt identifies a foundational example in Harriot's encounter with the Virginia Indians. See Stephen Greenblatt, "Invisible Bullets: Renaissance Authority and its Subversion, Henry IV and Henry V," in *Political Shakespeare: Essays in Cultural Materialism*, 2nd ed., ed. Jonathan Dollimore and Alan Sinfield (Ithaca, N.Y.: Cornell University Press, 1994), pp. 21–2. See also Herge, *Prisoners of the Sun* (Boston: Little, Brown, 1975), p. 59.

24. SD, p. 158.

25. SD, p. 158.

26. SD, p. 159.

27. SD, p. 159.

28. SD, p. 159.

29. Francis Jennings, *The Invasion of America: Indians, Colonialism, and the Cant of Conquest* (New York: W. W. Norton, 1976), pp. 128–45.

30. SD, p. 159.

31. See SD, Appendix XII, pp. 250–3, for the order appointing Warwick governor of the Committee for Foreign Plantations.

32. SD, Appendix II, p. 195–6.

33. SD, Appendix II, p. 196.

34. SD, Appendix II, p. 196.

35. Grantland Rice, *The Transformation of Authorship in America* (Chicago: University of Chicago Press, 1997), p. 5.

36. Rice, pp. 27, 29–30.

37. See Hill, pp. 58–60.

38. Samuel Gorton, "Letter to Nathaniel Morton," pp. 14–15.

39. Samuel Gorton, "Letter to Nathaniel Morton," p. 15.

40. JWJ, p. 703.

41. See JWJ, pp. 639–40, 650–2, 702–4, 701–2.

42. See Raymond P. Stearns, "The Weld–Peter mission to England," *Transactions of the Colonial Society of Massachusetts*, XXXII (1937): pp. 204–6.

43. See Barbara Donagan, "The Clerical Patronage of Robert Rich, Second Earl of Warwick, 1619–1642," in *Proceedings of the American Philosophical Society*, Vol. 120, no. 5, (1976), pp. 388–419.

44. David Underdown, *Pride's Purge: Politics in the Puritan Revolution* (London: George Allen and Unwin, 1985), pp. 208–56.

45. Underdown, pp. 220, 361–89.

46. J. H. Adamson and H. F. Holland, *Sir Harry Vane: His Life and Times, 1613–1662* (Boston: Gambit, 1973), pp. 241–4.

47. See Henry Plomer, *A dictionary of the booksellers and printers who were at work in England, Scotland and Ireland from 1641 to 1667* (London: For the Bibliographical Society, by Blades, East & Blades), 1907.

48. Philip Gura, "Samuel Gorton and Religious Radicalism in England 1644–48" *William and Mary Quarterly* 3rd Ser., Vol. 40, no. 1 (Jan. 1983), pp. 121–124.

49. David Hall, *Worlds of Wonder, Days of Judgment: Popular Religious Belief in Early New England* (Cambridge: Harvard University Press, 1989), p. 7.

50. See Mackie, pp. 380–1.

51. JWJ, p. 486.

52. Elizabeth Skerpan, *The Rhetoric of Politics in the English Revolution 1642–1660* (Columbia: University of Missouri Press, 1992), pp. 13–31; Nigel Smith, *Literature and Revolution in England 1640–1660* (New Haven, Conn.: Yale University Press, 1994), pp. 3–9.

4. ANTINOMIANS, ANABAPTISTS, AND AQUIDNECK:
Contesting Heresy in Interregnum London
(pp. 73–88)

1. William Coddington to John Cotton, Mar.–Apr. 1640/1, *Correspondence of John Cotton*, ed. Sargent Bush (Chapel Hill: Omohundro Institute of Early American History and Culture, Williamsburg, Virginia, by the University of North Carolina Press, 2001).

2. William Coddington to John Winthrop, 11 November 1646, in *The Winthrop Papers*, ed. Allyn B. Forbes (Boston: Massachusetts Historical Society, 1947), V: 118. This same letter contains a reference to a letter of October 1646, referring to Gorton, just after the return of Holden with Parliament's order.

3. Isaac Backus, *A History of New England with Particular Reference to Baptists*, 2 vols. (New York, Arno Press, 1969), pp. 169–70. For the United Colonies, see Harry M. Ward, *The United Colonies of New England, 1643–90* (New York: Vantage Press, 1961).

4. See Jeremy Belknap, *The History of New Hampshire* (Dover, N.H.: George Wadleigh, 1862), pp. 17–34.

5. *Ill Newes from New England*, 6. Hereafter abbreviated as INFNE.

6. *Calendar of State Papers, Colonial, 1574–1660*, pp. 335–8, 353–4; *Newport Historical Society, Bulletin*, No. 44, pp. 9–13; Glenn LaFantasie, ed., *The Correspondence of Roger Williams* (Hanover, N.H., and London: Brown University Press/ University Press of New England, 1988), I: 332–3. Hereafter abbreviated as CRW.

7. For this trip see O'Toole, p. 448; *Correspondence of Roger Williams*, I: 303–4. For the margins of Plymouth as a target for religious dissidents, see Foster, *The Long Argument*, p. 190.

8. James, p. 45.

9. INFNE, [xv].

10. INFNE, [xviii].

11. See chapter 5.

12. INFNE, p. 19. Holmes's sentence appears on p. 16.

13. This comparison of the persecutions of Laud to the excesses of the Bay Colony was not unique to Clarke, and it would also become a staple of Quaker discourse about the Bay Colony. For a description of the Marian persecution and Foxe's accounts of them, see Haller, pp. 19–47; for the evolution of an English Protestant discourse of martyrdom from Eusebius' history of primitive Christianity, see Knott, pp. 33–46.

14. See [William Prynne], *A New Discovery of the Prelates Tyranny* (London: 1641).

15. Elizabeth Skerpan, *The Rhetoric of Politics in the English Revolution, 1642–1660* (Columbia: University of Missouri Press, 1992), p. 43.

16. David Cressy, *Travesties and Transgressions in Tudor and Stuart England* (Oxford: Oxford University Press, 2000), p. 222.

17. Knott, p. 140.

18. Knott, p. 4; see also Achinstein, pp. 43–4.

19. Cressy, pp. 226–30.

20. See Knott, pp. 144–50.

21. Henry Jessey to John Winthrop 18 August, [1637] in the *Winthrop Papers*, in *Collections of the Massachusetts Historical Society* [hereafter CMHS], 4th Ser., Vol. VI, p. 464. This correspondence dates back to at least 1629, when the two men were in closer sympathy: In 1647, the last surviving letter from Jessey to Winthrop reproaches him for Massachusetts's new law against Anabaptists (CMHS, 4th Ser., Vol. VI, p. 446).

22. Skerpan, p. 45.

23. See INFNE, pp. 9–12.

24. [William Prynne], *A Briefe Relation of Certaine Speciall and Most Materiall Passages and Speeches in the Starre Chamber . . .* [(London: for M.S., 1641]), p. 47. This text, a greatly expanded version of a 1638 text of the same name, appears at the conclusion of [William Prynne], *A New Discovery of the Prelates Tyranny* (London: for M.S., 1641). *New Discovery* and *Briefe Relation* were issued together, but paginated separately.

25. INFNE, p. 19.

26. *Briefe Relation*, p. 52.

27. INFNE, p. 19.

28. INFNE, 19–20; *Briefe Relation*, p. 46.

29. Knott observes that Burton "displays the strongest sense of the dramatic potential of his role" among these three convicts" (p. 141).

30. INFNE, p. 21.

31. According to Edward Rossingham, who described the event in a manuscript newsletter, Burton described the pillory as the "happiest pulpit he had ever preached in." As quoted in Cressy, p. 225.

32. INFNE, p. 22.

33. INFNE, p. 21.

34. INFNE, p. 22.

35. *Briefe Relation*, p. 49.

36. *Briefe Relation*, p. 56.

37. Knott, p. 140.

38. See INFNE, pp. 26–29.

39. *Briefe Relation*, p. 59. It is curious to see this avowedly Protestant discourse producing the kind of veneration of corporeal relics more typically associated with Roman Catholicism.

40. *Briefe Relation*, pp. 91–100. For an account of Prynne's trip through Chester, see Cressy, pp. 226–9.

41. Knott, p. 134.

42. INFNE, pp. 39, 49, 60, 62.

43. See *The Confession of Faith of Those Churches Which Are Commonly Though Falsly Called Anabaptist* (London: Matthew Simmons, 1644), p. 3. For a complete list of the signers of both the 1644 and 1644 confessions, see Murray Tolmie, *The Triumph of the Saints: The Separate Churches of London, 1616–1649* (Cambridge: Cambridge University Press, 1977), p. 58.

44. DNB "William Kiffin." CD-ROM (Oxford: Oxford University Press, 1997).

45. See Tolmie, pp. 7–19.

46. Tolmie, p. 18.

47. William Kiffin, *The Life and Death of That Old Disciple of Christ and Eminent Minister of the Gospel, Mr. Hanserd Knollys* (London: for John Harris, 1692), p. 17.

48. For a précis of Knollys's career in New Hampshire, see Belknap, pp. 26–7.

49. *Life and Death of Hanserd Knollys*, pp. 12, 10.

50. Cromwell is reputed to have claimed to have been "more afraid of meeting Wheelwright at foot-ball, than of meeting any army since in the field, for he was infallably sure of being tript up by him." Belknap, p. 32, quoting Cotton Mather.

51. Interregnum Entry Book, Col. CIV, p. 214; Calendar of State Papers (1574–1660) p. 427, as quoted in Richard LeBaron Bowen, *The Providence Oath of Allegiance and its Signers, 1651–2* (Providence, R.I.: Society of Colonial Wars, 1943), p. 40.

52. See Henry Plomer, *A dictionary of the booksellers and printers who were at work in England, Scotland and Ireland from 1641 to 1667* (London: For the Bibliographical Society, by Blades, East & Blades), 1907.

53. See W. T. Whitley, "The English Career of John Clarke, Rhode Island,"

Baptist Quarterly, Vol. 1 (1922), pp. 368–72. After this possible dalliance with the Fifth Monarchists, and after the Restoration, Clarke did more work on behalf of the colony, successfully petitioning Charles II for the 1663 charter that served as the frame of Rhode Island's government for almost two centuries. The most accessible account of this campaign is in James, pp. 59–84.

54. *Correspondence of Roger Williams*, I: 356; Vane's influence largely disappeared in April 1653 with Cromwell's dissolution of the Rump, but it is reasonable to imagine that he helped Williams's and Clarke's suit gain momentum before then.

55. *Correspondence of Roger Williams*, II: 393; See also Masson, IV: 528–9.

56. *Correspondence of John Cotton*, p. 497. Saltonstall's letter also appears in *The Saltonstall Papers*, which offers a useful biography of Saltonstall but does not include Cotton's response.

57. "Sir Richard Saltonstall," in *The Saltonstall Papers. Collections of the Massachusetts Historical Society*, No. 80 (Boston: 1972), pp. 7–8.

58. *The Humble Request of His Majesties Loyall Subjects, the Governour and Company Late Gone for New-England . . .* (London: for John Bellamie, 1630), p. 10.

59. "Sir Richard Saltonstall," pp. 11–12.

60. *Correspondence of John Cotton*, pp. 497–8.

61. Samuel Eliot Morison, *Builders of the Bay Colony*, revised and enlarged ed. (Boston: Houghton Mifflin, 1964), pp. 33–4.

62. *Calendar of State Papers, Colonial*, I: 377.

63. LaFantasie, I: 362.

64. *Calendar of State Papers, Colonial*, I: 390.

65. The complete transcription of this order is in Bowen, p. 40.

66. Bowen, p. 40; several members of this Council of State had interested themselves in Williams and Gorton's earlier suits. The members of this body with a demonstrated interest in colonial affairs include Cromwell himself; Sir Arthur Hasselrig, Bart.; Sir William Masham, Bart.; Sir Gilbert Pickering, Bart.; Sir Henry Mildmay, Kt.; Sir Henry Vane, Kt.; Henry Rolle, Chief Justice Upper Bench; Oliver. St. John, Chief Justice Common Bench; Bulstrode Whitlocke, Council at Law; Col. William Purefoy; Dennis Bond, Esq.; Cornelius Holland, Esq.; Ald. Isaac Pennington; and Major Richard Salwey. The complete composition of the various configurations of the Council of State is detailed in Masson, Vol. VI.

67. Oliver Cromwell to "Our trusty and well-beloved President, Assistants, and Inhabitants of Rhode Island, together with the rest of the Providence Plantations . . . . 29 March 1655" in *The Writings and Speeches of Oliver Cromwell*, ed. Wilbur Cortez Abbot (Cambridge: Cambridge University Press, 1988), p. 681.

5. SUFFERING AND SUBSCRIBING:
Configurations of Authorship in the Quaker Atlantic
(pp. 90–114)

1. Humphrey Norton, *New-England's Ensigne* (London: By T.L. for G. Calvert 1660), t.p.

2. Michel Foucault, "What is an Author?," in *The Foucault Reader*, ed. Paul Rabinow (New York: Pantheon, 1984), p. 108.

3. Roger Chartier points out that focusing on penal responsibility emphasizes the sixteenth century, while focusing on proprietary claims in the literary marketplace emphasizes the eighteenth; as such, the seventeenth century suggests itself as an era when the figure of the author was perhaps more malleable than before or after. Roger Chartier, *The Order of Books: Readers, Authors, and Libraries in Europe between the Fourteenth and Eighteenth Centuries*, trans. Lydia G. Cochrane (Stanford, Calif.: Stanford University Press, 1994), n. 35, p. 104.

4. Norton, *New-England's Ensigne*, t.p.

5. Frederick Tolles, *Quakers and the Atlantic Culture* (New York, MacMillan, 1960), p. 27; Kate Peters, *Print Culture and the Early Quakers* (Cambridge, Cambridge University Press, 2005), pp. 11–12; for an overview of key documents in the debate over the status of radical sects in the 1650s, see Peters, pp. 5–6.

6. Peters, pp. 252–5.

7. Carla Pestana, *The English Atlantic in an Age of Revolution* (Cambridge, Mass.: Harvard University Press, 2004), p. 147.

8. Carla Pestana, *Quakers and Baptists in Colonial Massachusetts* (Cambridge, Mass.: Cambridge University Press, 1991), pp. 34–8.

9. Knott, p. 218.

10. See William Haller, *Foxe's Book of Martyrs and the Elect Nation* (London: J. Cape, 1963), passim.

11. Indeed, Foxe's identification as author with the narratives of martyrdom was strong enough that his *Acts and Monuments* was widely referred to as "Foxe's Book of Martyrs."

12. Elaine Scarry, *The Body in Pain: The Making and Unmaking of the World* (Oxford: Oxford University Press, 1985), pp. 27–59, esp. pp. 35, 54.

13. Janel Mueller, "Pain, Persecution and the Construction of Selfhood in Foxe's *Acts and Monuments*," in *Religion and Culture in Renaissance England*, ed. Claire McEachern and Debora Shuger (Cambridge: Cambridge University Press, 1997), pp. 165–6.

14. Scarry, p. 29.

15. Referring to a colony as "the state" is obviously problematic, especially in a transatlantic context. However, the very act of appropriating the state's monopoly

on legitimate violence for itself is a significant part of Quaker protests against the New England colonies.

16. *Dictionary of National Biography*, s.v. "Howgill, Francis."

17. Francis Howgill, *The Popish Inquisition Newly Erected in New-England* . . . (London: Thomas Simmons, 1659), p. A2.

18. *Popish Inquisition*, p. A2.

19. *Popish Inquisition*, p. [A3].

20. *Popish Inquisition*, p. 25.

21. *Popish Inquisition*, pp. 26–27.

22. Round, p. 49.

23. Michel Foucault, *Discipline and Punish: The Birth of the Prison*, trans. Alan Sheridan (New York, Vintage Books, 1979), p. 49.

24. Foucault, *Discipline and Punish*, p. 9.

25. *Popish Inquisition*, pp. 27–8.

26. *Popish Inquisition*, p. 28.

27. *Popish Inquisition*, p. 61.

28. *Popish Inquisition*, p. 43.

29. *Popish Inquisition*, pp. 43–4.

30. Peters, p. 175.

31. [Humphrey Norton,] *New-England's Ensigne* (London: G. Calvert, 1659), t.p.

32. *New-England's Ensigne*, p. 24; a similar technique appears in *New England Judged*, p. 194.

33. *New-England's Ensigne*, pp. 1–2.

34. *New-England's Ensigne*, p. 4.

35. For a detailed study of the evolution of experience as a narrative trope in colonial discourse, see Jim Egan, *Authorizing Experience: Refigurations of the Body Politic in Seventeenth-Century New England Writing* (Princeton, N.J.: Princeton University Press, 1999), esp. chap. 2.

36. Knott, p. 218.

37. Edward Burrough, *A Declaration of the Sad and Great Persecution. . .* (London: 1661), p. 29; George Bishop, *New England Judged* [I] (London, 1661), p. 50.

38. Thomas Underhill, *Hell Broke Loose, Or An History of the Quakers* (London: For Simon Miller, 1660); Cotton Mather, *Magnalia Christii Americana* (Hartford: 1853), II: p. 504.

39. *New-England's Ensigne*, p. 57.

40. Richard Bauman, *Let Your Words be Few: Symbolism of Speaking and Silence among Seventeenth-Century Quakers* (Cambridge: Cambridge University Press, 1983), p. 104.

41. Sharon Achinstein, *Milton and the Revolutionary Reader* (Princeton, N.J.: Princeton University Press, 1994), p. 36. Achinstein also notes that Lilburne an-

ticipated a classic Quaker gesture by some years in his refusal to remove his hat before Parliament (p. 36).

42. *New-England's Ensigne*, p. 93.

43. Barbara Ritter Daley, "The early Quaker mission and the settlement of meetings in Barbados 1655–1700," *Journal of the Barbados Museum and Historical Society*, 39 (1991), especially pp. 27–30.

44. *New England Judged*, pp. 197–8.

45. "A Declaration of the General Court of The Massachusetts Holden at Boston October 18 1659 Concerning the Execution of Two Quakers" (Reprint, London: 1659); see Bishop, *New England Judged*, pp. 34–7, for a critique of this notion of a "back door."

46. Marmaduke Stephenson, *A Call from Death to Life* (London: for Thomas Simmons, 1660), p. [4].

47. *A Call*, p. 5.

48. *A Call*, p. 5.

49. *A Call*, p. 11.

50. *A Call*, p. 25.

51. *A Call*, p. 25.

52. *A Call*, p. 30.

53. As quoted in Mueller, p. 171.

54. *A Call*, p. 30.

55. Sewel, *The History of the Rise, Increase, and Progress of the Christian People Called Quakers* (New York: Baker & Clarke, 1844), I: 345.

56. *New England Judged*, p. 141.

57. See *New England Judged*, pp. 93–5. (Page 97 is mispaginated as p. 89, producing two page 93s. The narrative of Stephenson and Robinson begins on the first p. 93.)

58. See *A Call*, pp. 21–4; *New England Judged*, pp. 95–[106].

59. *New England Judged*, pp. 107–8.

60. *New England Judged*, pp. 177–94.

61. Sewel, I: 345.

62. *A Declaration*, p. 19.

63. *A Declaration*, p. 20.

64. Sewel, I: 345.

65. *Calendar of State Papers, Colonial Series*, Vol. V, number 168. See also Jones, p. 90.

CONCLUSION:
"A Lively Experiment"
(pp. 116–126)

1. Rhode Island was the first to proclaim the new King, while Massachusetts delayed this recognition for months.

2. For the trajectory of experience as a source of authority see Egan, pp. 32–46.

3. James, p. 67.

4. *Records of the Colony of Rhode Island*, 10 vols, ed. John Russell Bartlett (Providence: 1856–65), I: 486. Hereafter abbreviated RCRI.

5. RCRI, I: 486.

6. Dictionary of National Biography, "William Kiffin" (CD-ROM edition, Oxford University Press, 1997).

7. Edward, Earl of Clarendon, *The History of the Rebellion and Civil Wars in England* (Oxford: 1888), XV: 106; see also Thomas Crosby, *The History of the English Baptists* (London: 1738), I: 250.

8. RCRI, I: 486.

9. RCRI, I: 488.

10. RCRI, I: 488.

11. RCRI, I: 490.

12. RCRI, I: 491.

13. The Rhode Island charter was robust and sound enough to serve as the frame of the state's government even after English control of the colony ceased. The charter survived as the foundation of the state's governance until 1843, when it was superceded by the present constitution.

14. Charter.

15. Charter.

16. Charter.

17. Charter.

18. Charter.

19. Charter.

20. INFNE, p. 78.

21. *Oxford English Dictionary*, 2nd ed., s.v. "Experiment." The two quotations bracketing Clarke's usage are illustrative: C. 1645 Howell Lett. (1650) II. 113, I know by som experiments which I have had of you. 1699 Bentley Phal. Pref. 4, I speak from Experiment. Cf. Sense 6: "Practical proof; a specimen, an example. 1628 Preston New Covt. (1634) 302, I will give you an experiment of it; you shall see two notable examples of it." It is also worth noting that in a contemporary use of "experiment" as a verb, it is defined as "To have experience of; to experience; to feel, suffer. Obs.1503 Sheph. Kalender lii, He shall . . experyment evill fortunes.

1659 Hammond On Ps. iii. 7 Paraphr. 23 Thy fatherly mercy . . so often experi-
mented by me."

    22. Charter.

    23. Charter.

    24. Charter.

    25. Charter.